JESUS DAYS

1978 - 1983

Greg Reynolds

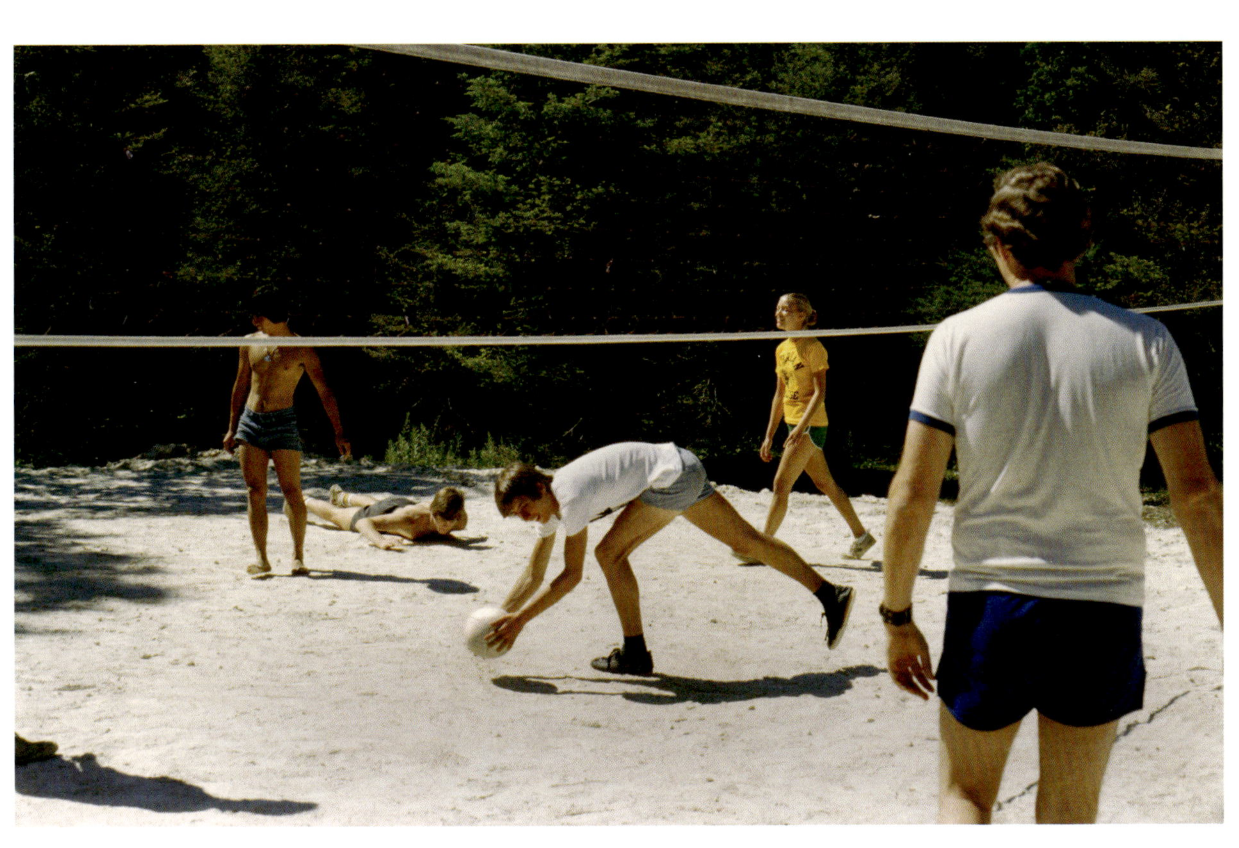

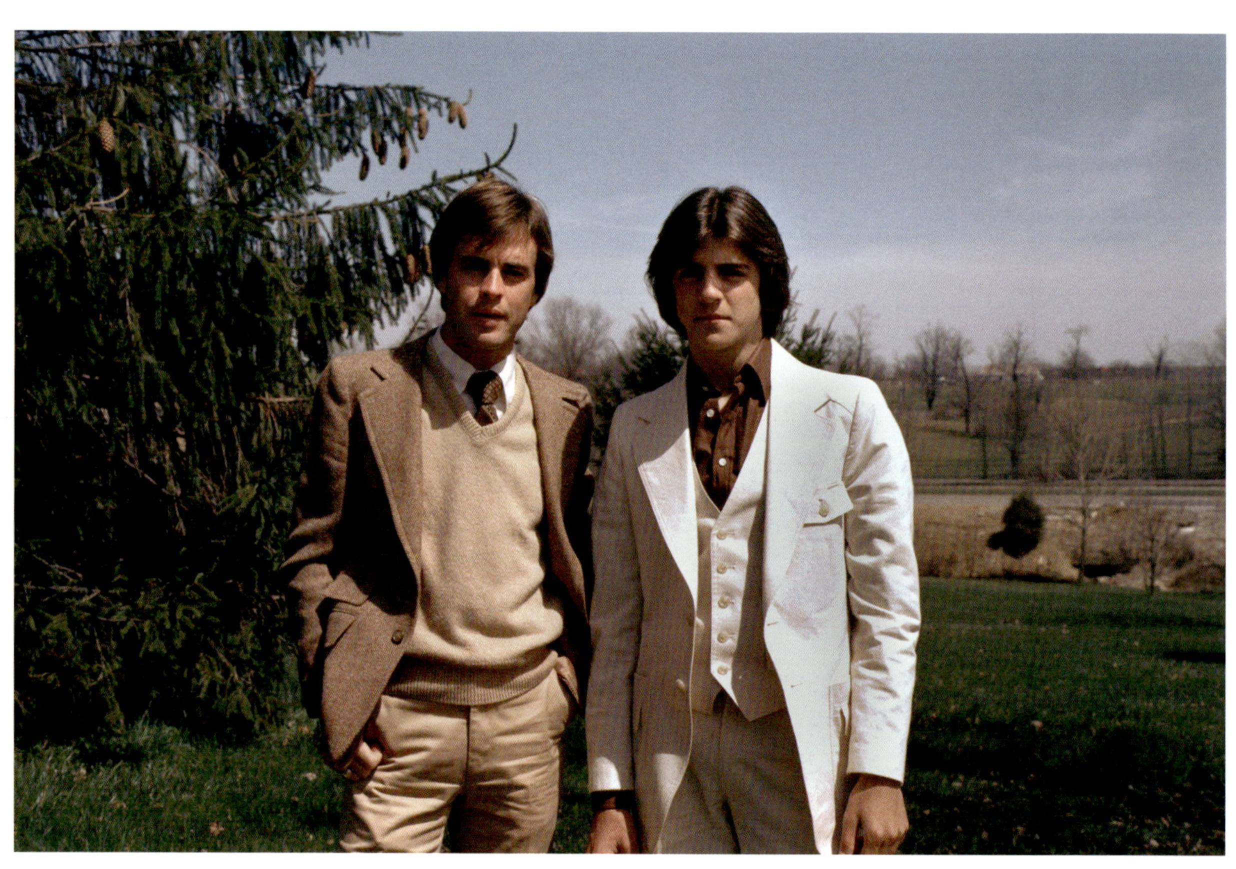

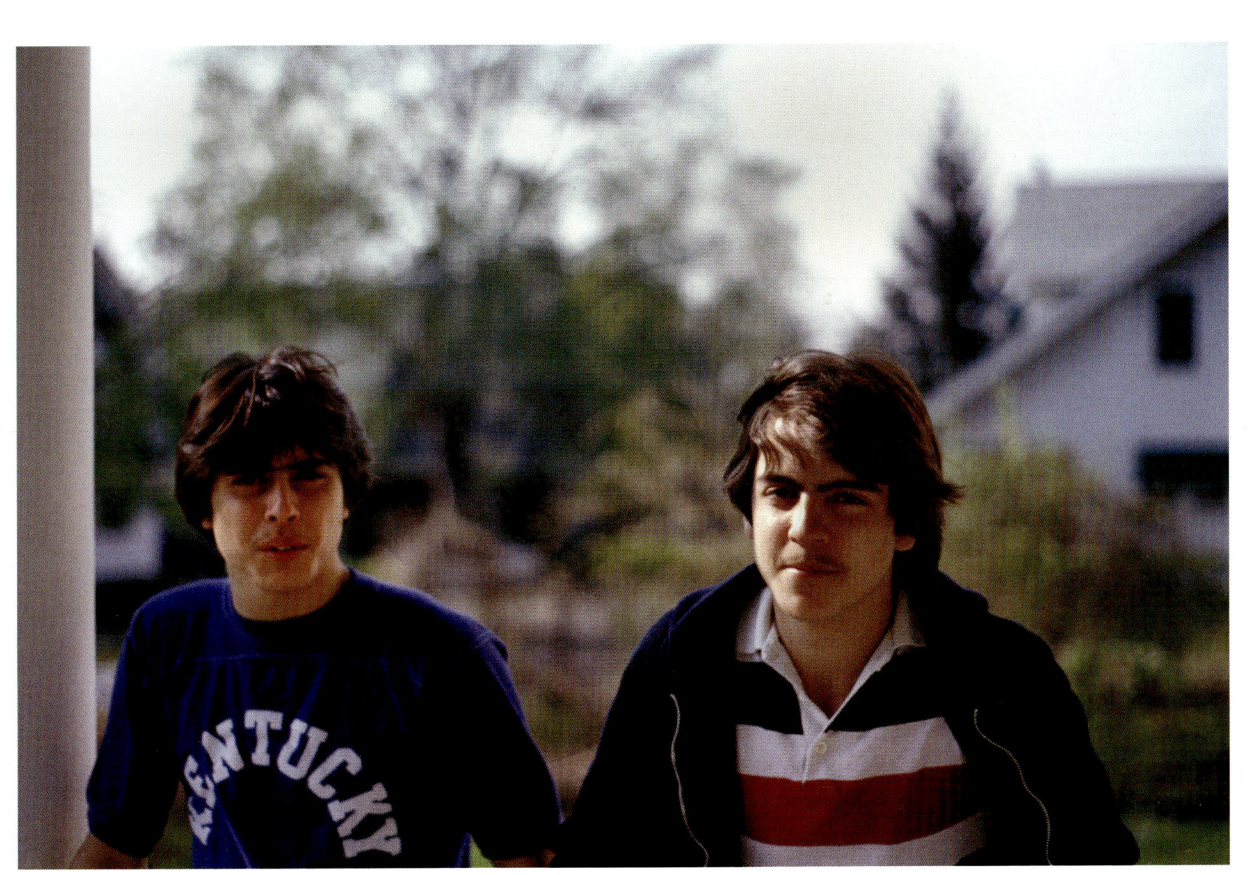

KENTUCKY

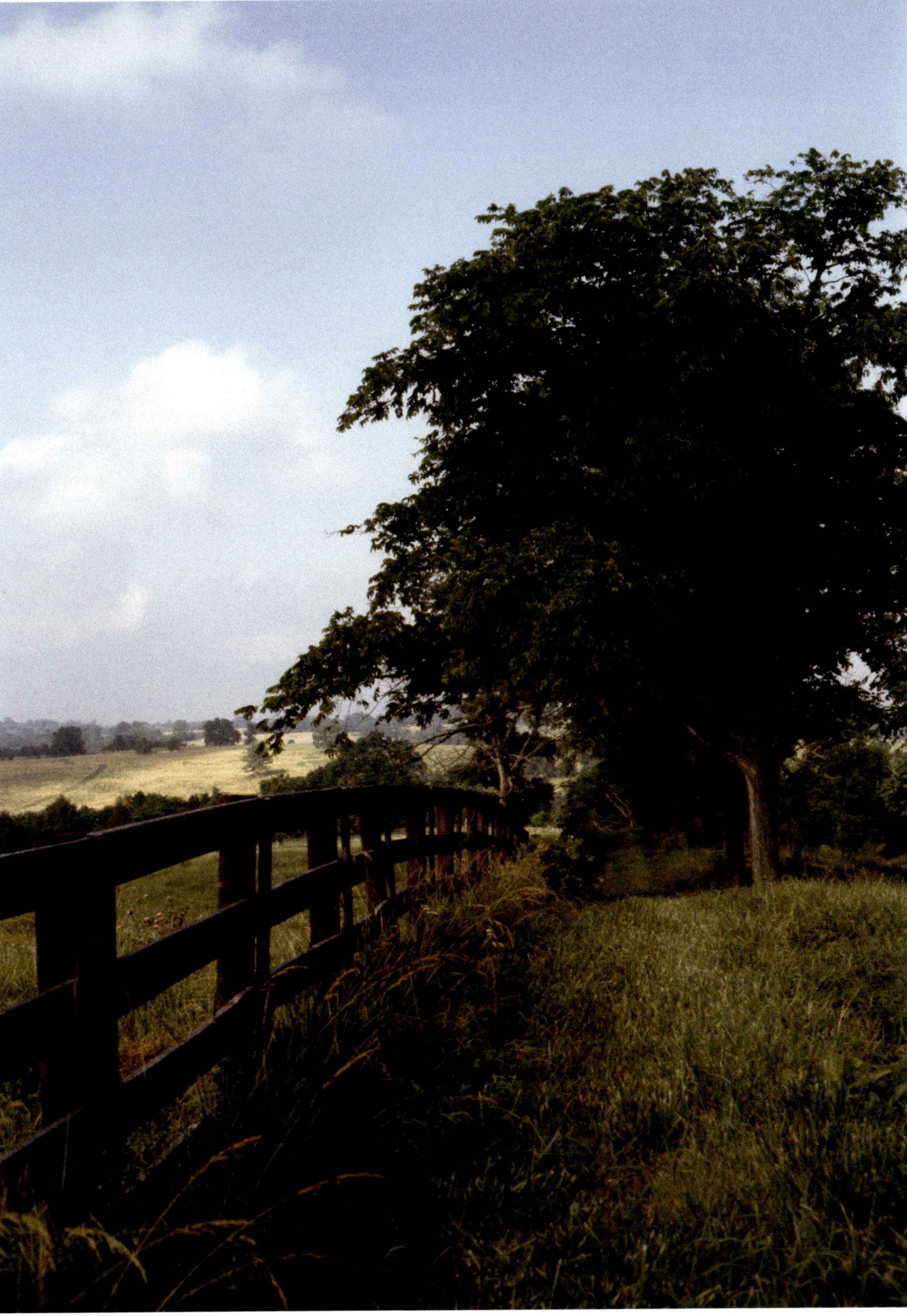

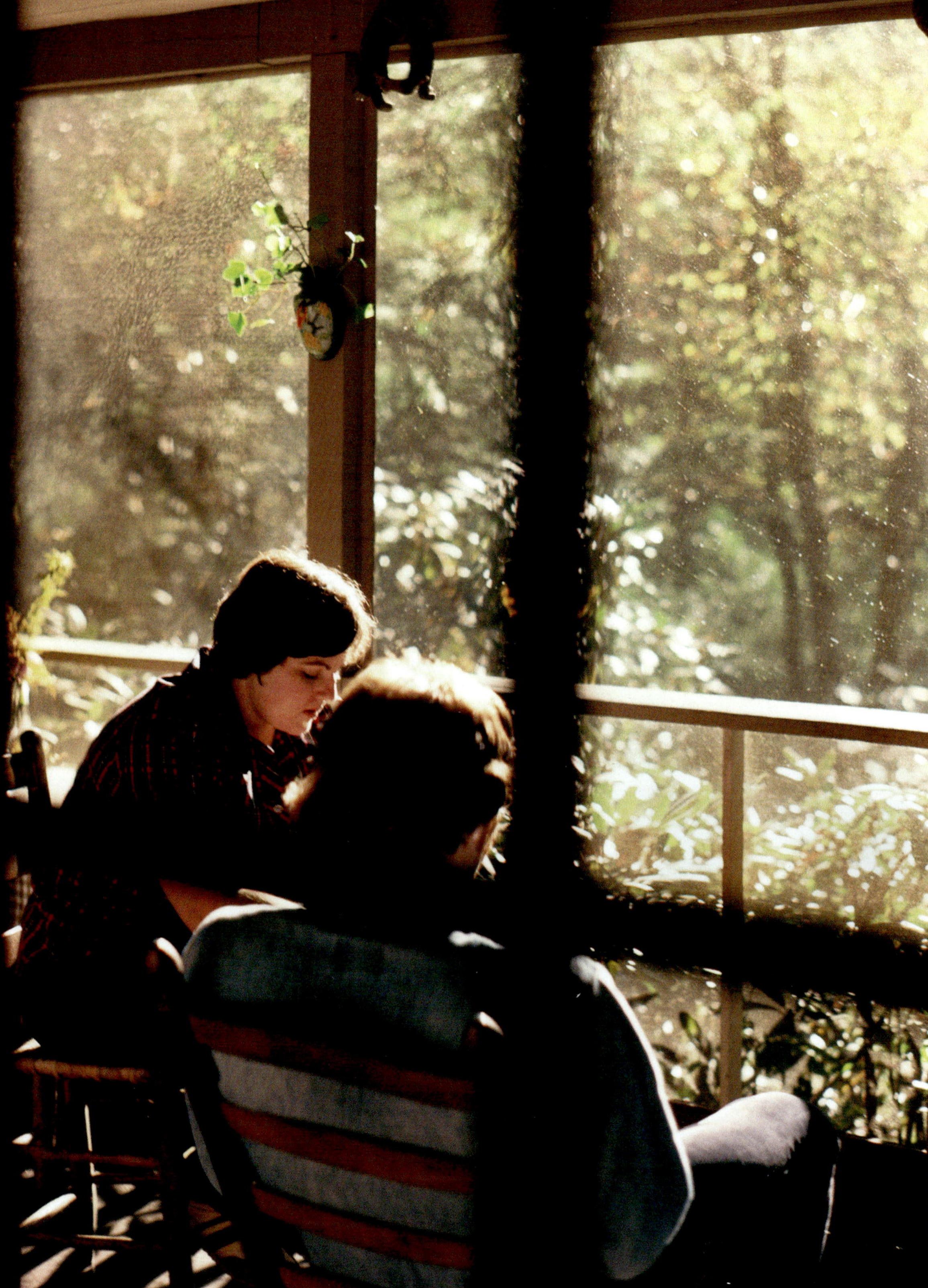

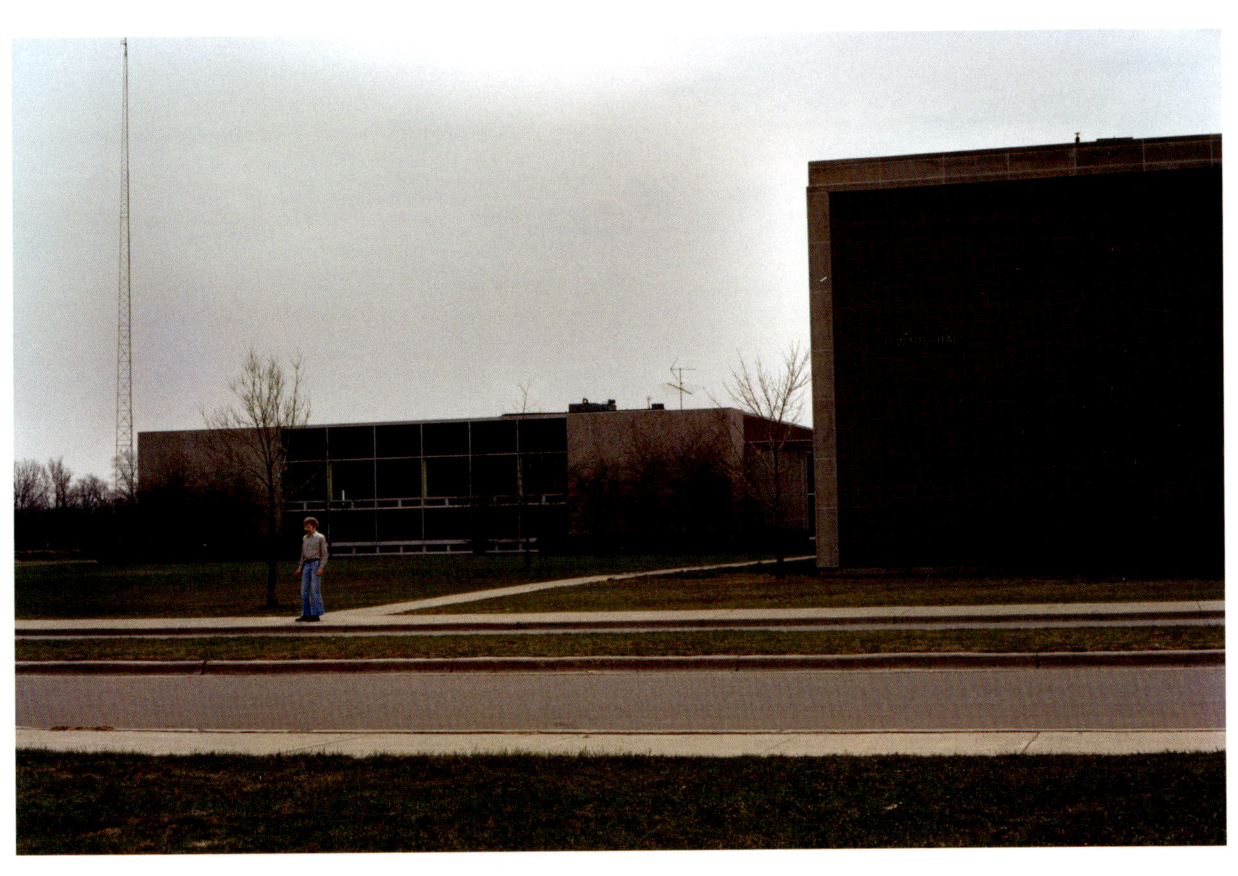

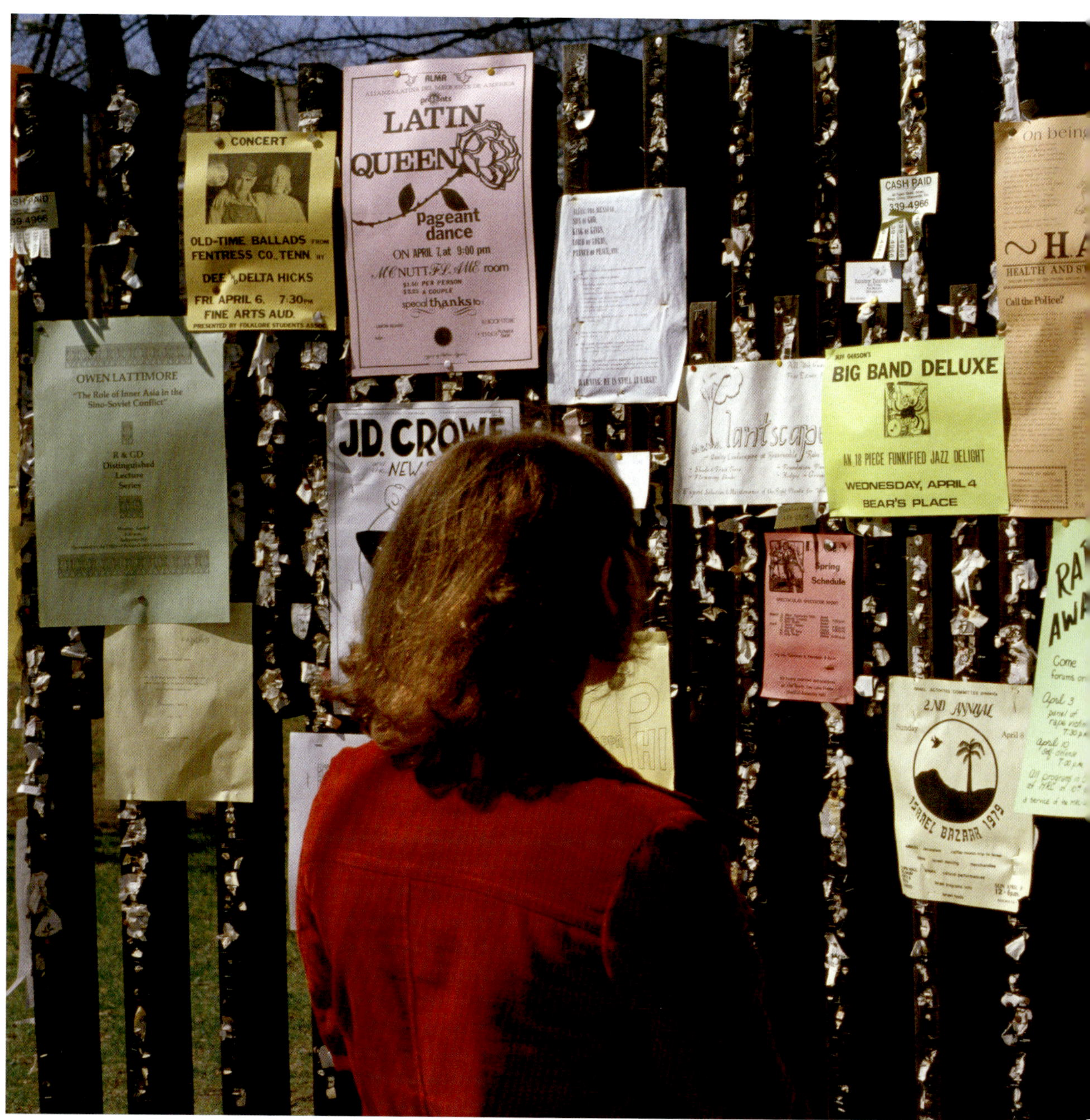
CONCERT
OLD-TIME BALLADS FROM FENTRESS CO., TENN. BY
DEE & DELTA HICKS
FRI. APRIL 6. 7:30 PM
FINE ARTS AUD.
PRESENTED BY FOLKLORE STUDENTS ASSOC.

ALMA
ALIANZA LATINA DEL SUDOESTE DE AMERICA
presents
LATIN QUEEN
pageant dance
ON APRIL 7, at 9:00 pm
McNUTT FL AME room
$3.00 PER PERSON
$5.00 A COUPLE
special thanks to:

CASH PAID
339-4966

On being
~ HA
HEALTH AND S
Call the Police

OWEN LATTIMORE
"The Role of Inner Asia in the Sino-Soviet Conflict"
R & GD
Distinguished
Lecture
Series

J.D. CROWE
NEW

lantscape

BIG BAND DELUXE
AN 18 PIECE FUNKIFIED JAZZ DELIGHT
WEDNESDAY, APRIL 4
BEAR'S PLACE

Spring
Schedule

RA
AWA
Come
forums on
April 3
April 6
April 10

2ND ANNUAL
ISRAEL BAZAAR 1979

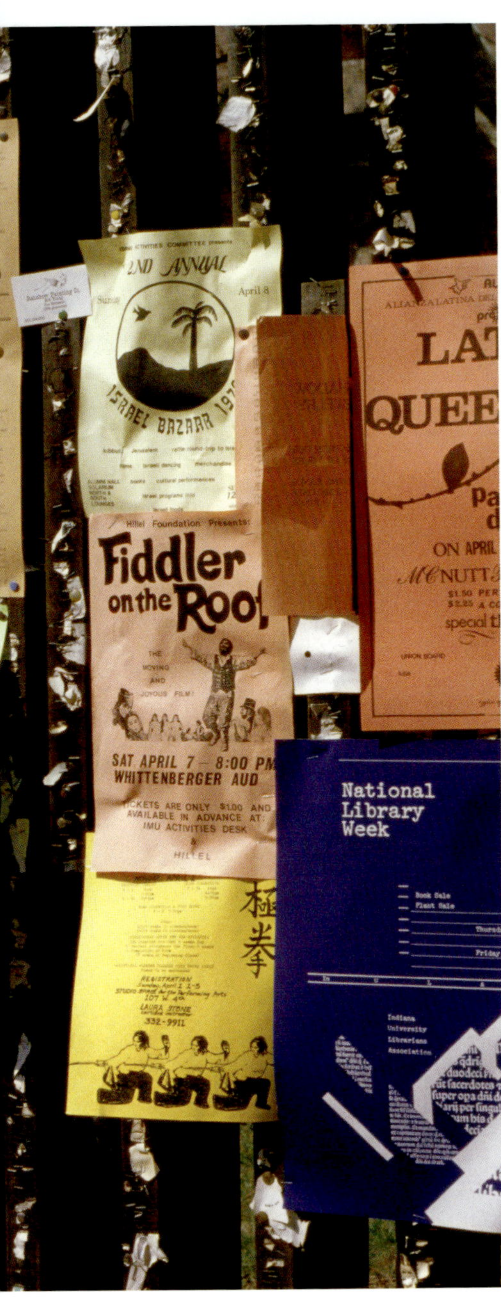
2ND ANNUAL
Sun April 8
ISRAEL BAZAAR 197
Hillel Foundation Presents
Fiddler
on the Roof
THE MOVING AND JOYOUS FILM!
SAT APRIL 7 — 8:00 PM
WHITTENBERGER AUD
TICKETS ARE ONLY $1.00 AND
AVAILABLE IN ADVANCE AT
IMU ACTIVITIES DESK
HILLEL
ALIANZA LATINA
LAT
QUEE
ON APRIL
McNUTT
$1.50 PER
$2.25 A CO
special th
UNION BOARD
REGISTRATION
Sunday, April 1 1-5
STUDIO Brown Ave. the Performing Arts
LOT W 4th
LAURA STONE
332-9911
National
Library
Week
Book Sale
Plant Sale
Thursd
Friday
Indiana
University
Librarians
Association

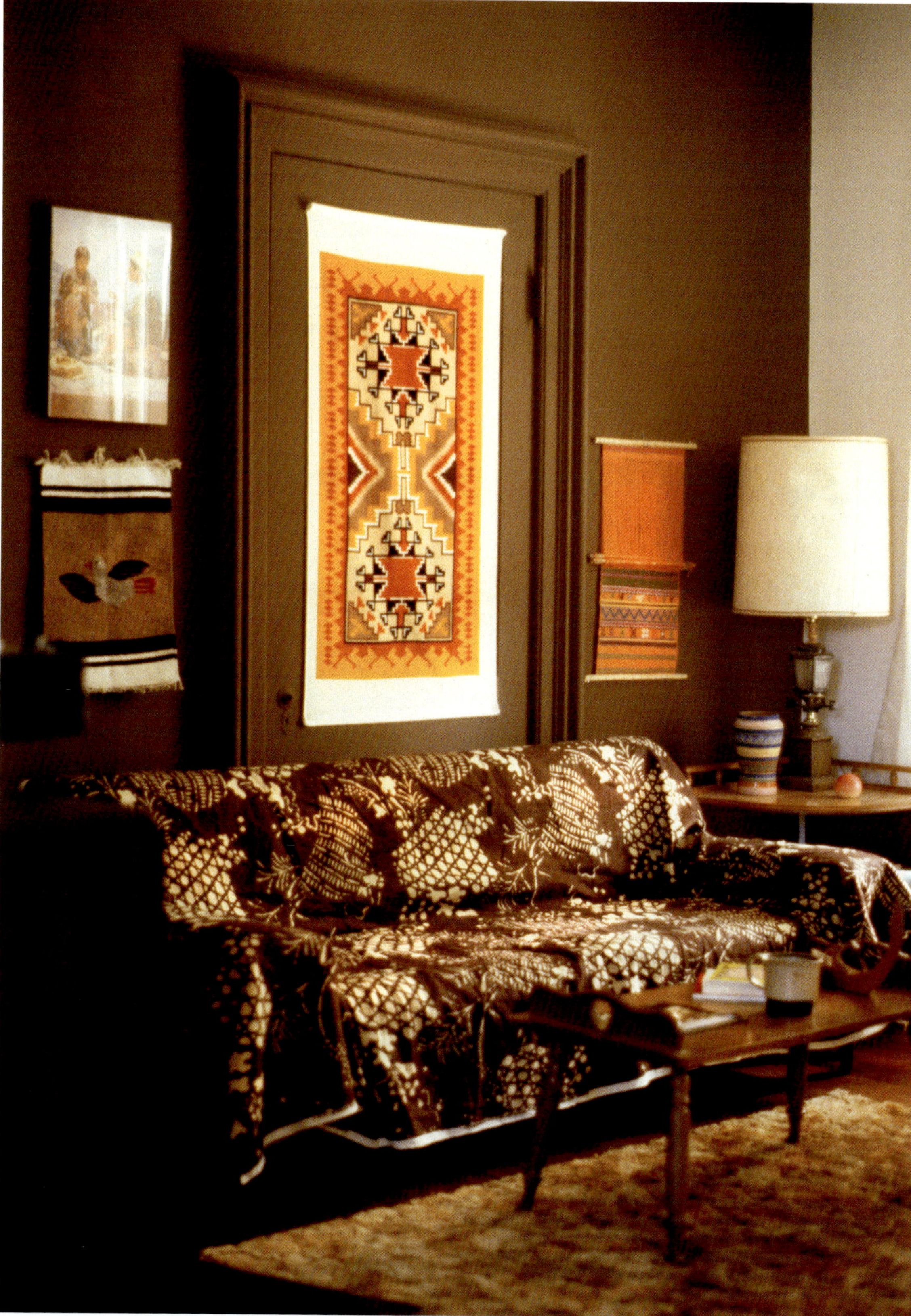

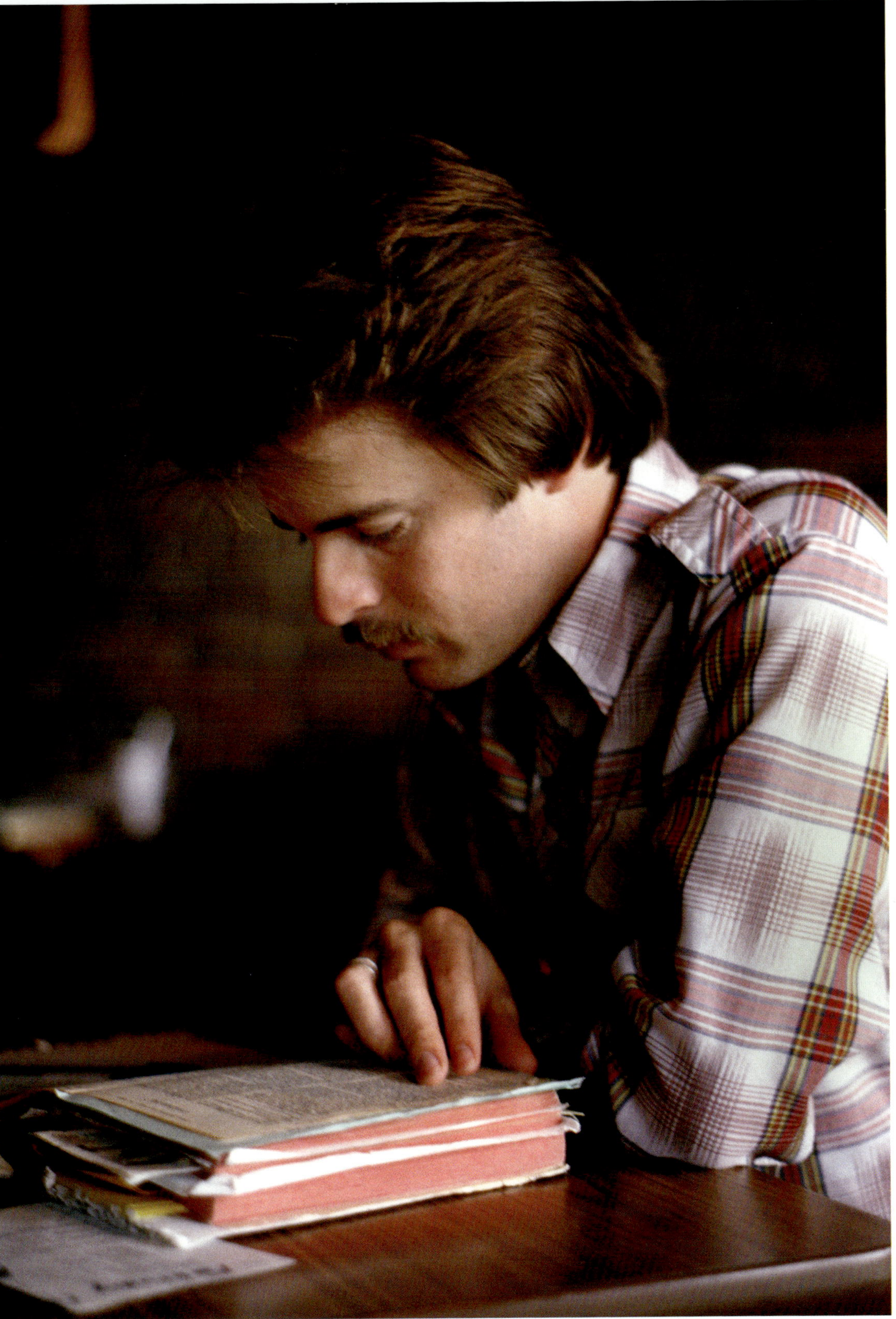

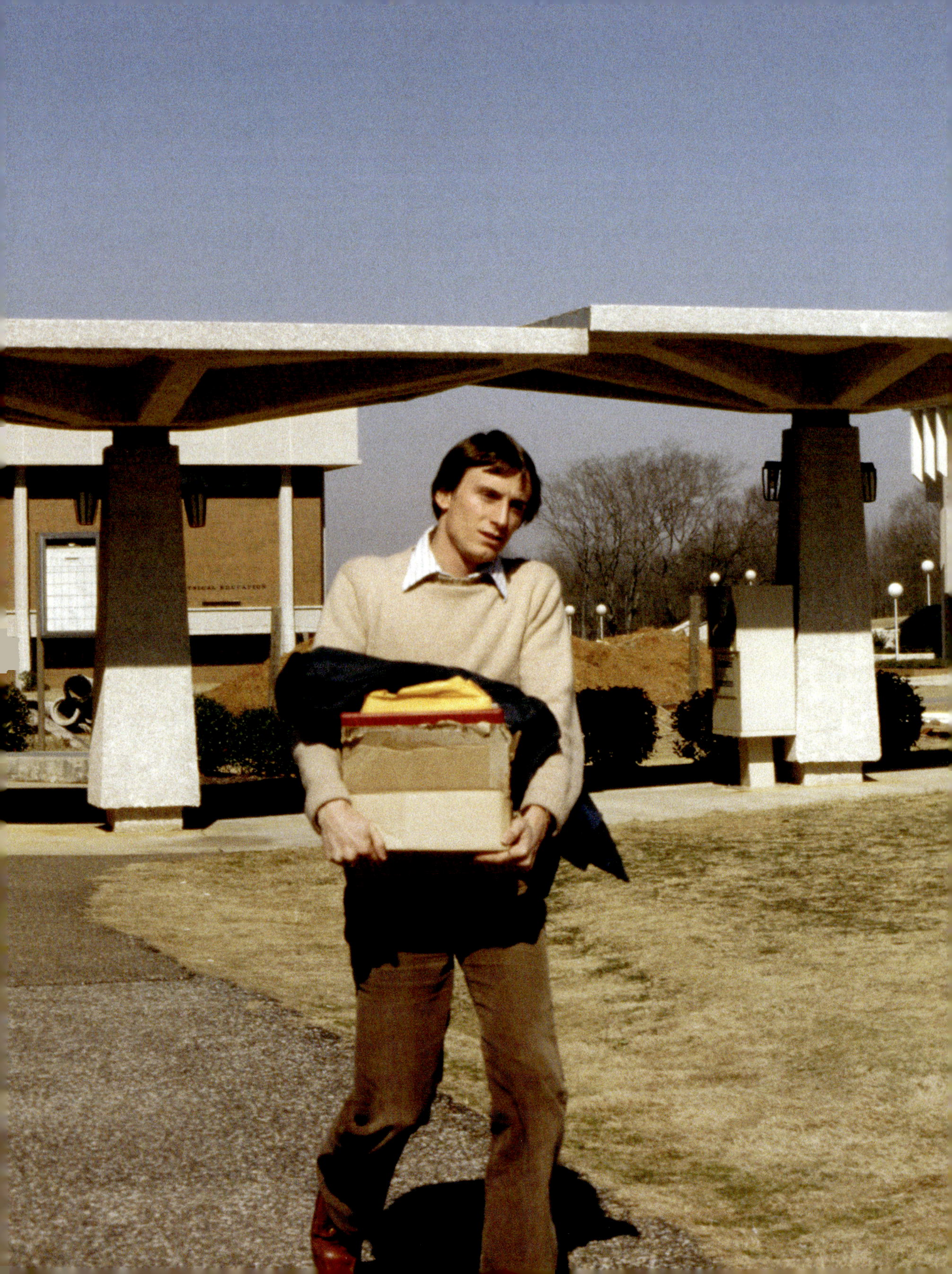

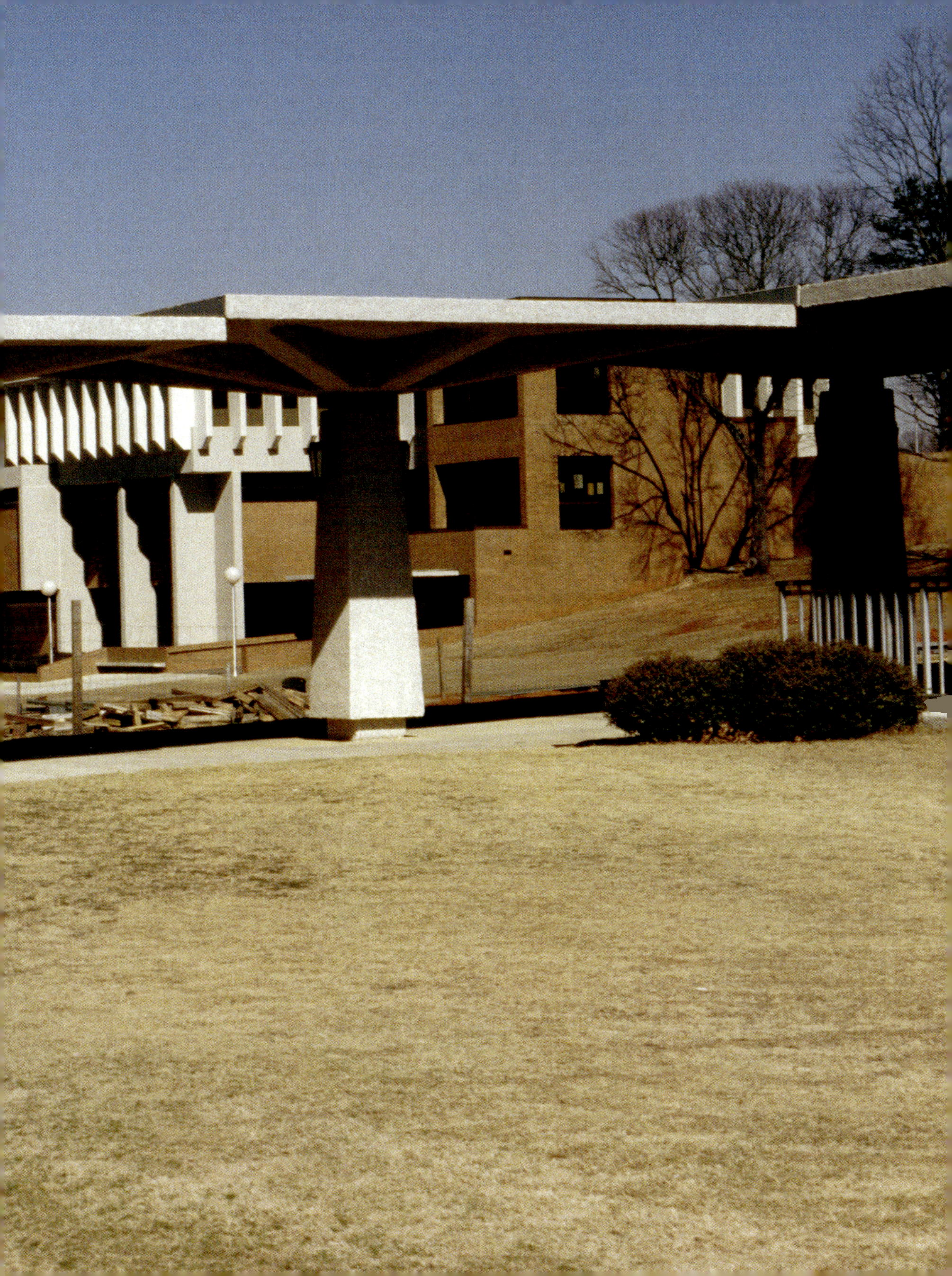

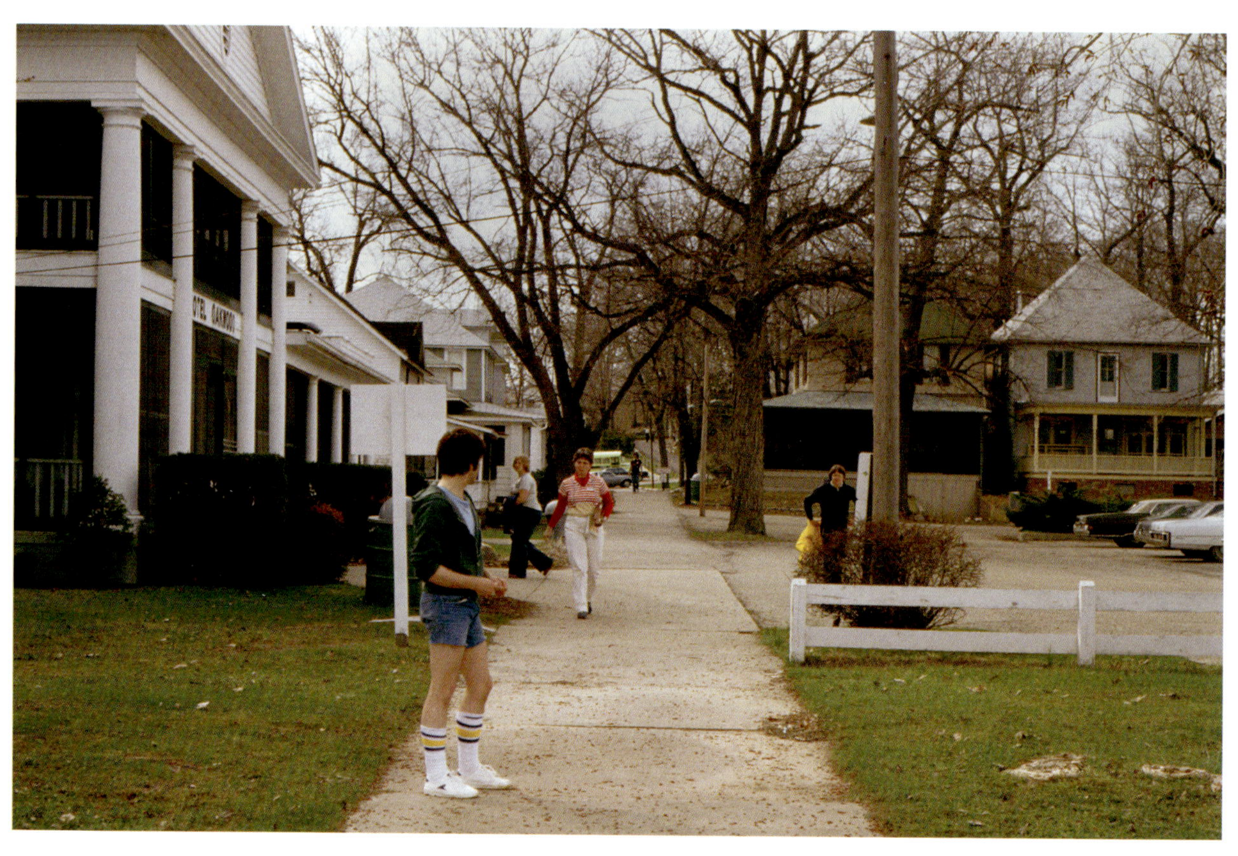

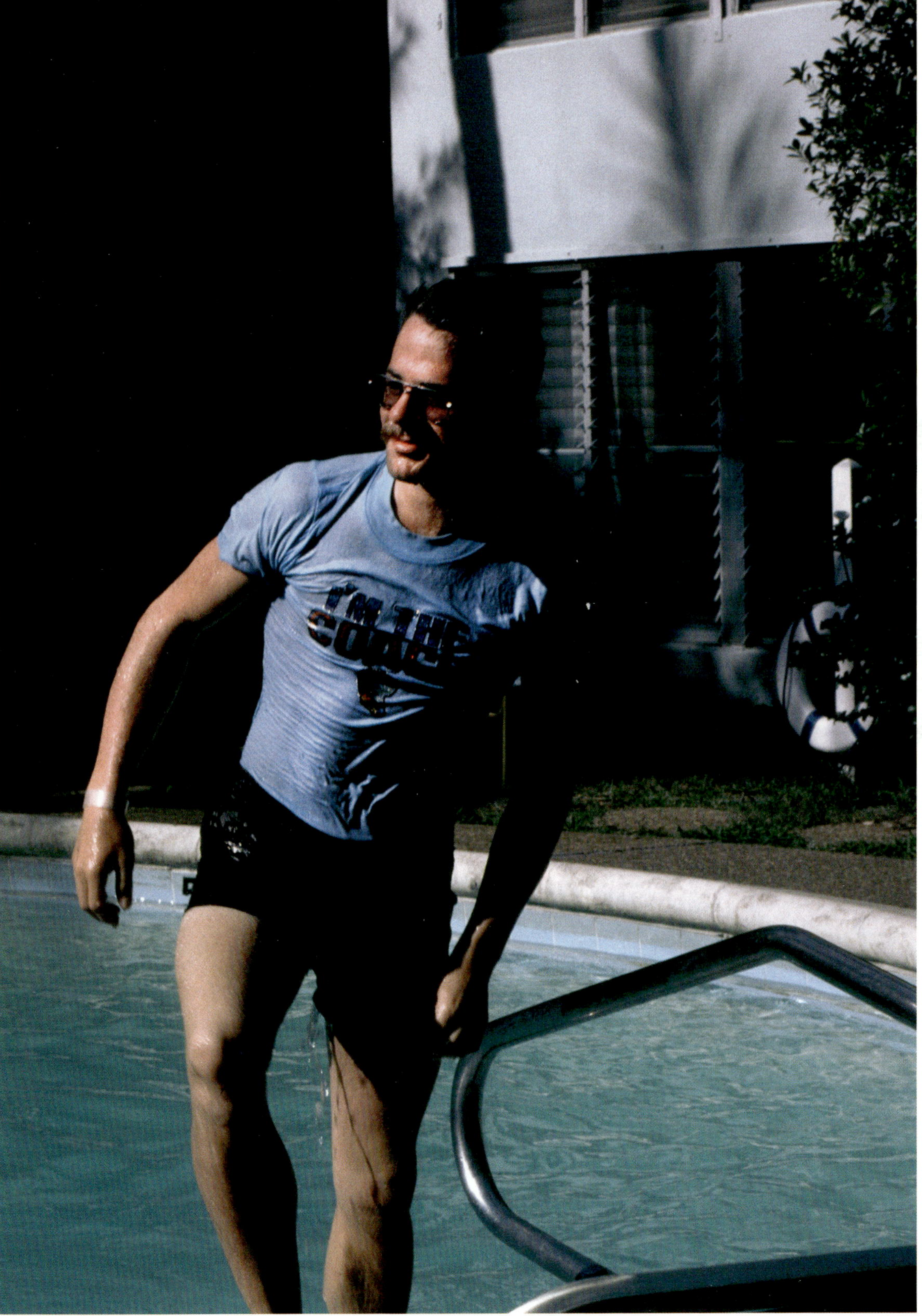
I'M THE
COACH

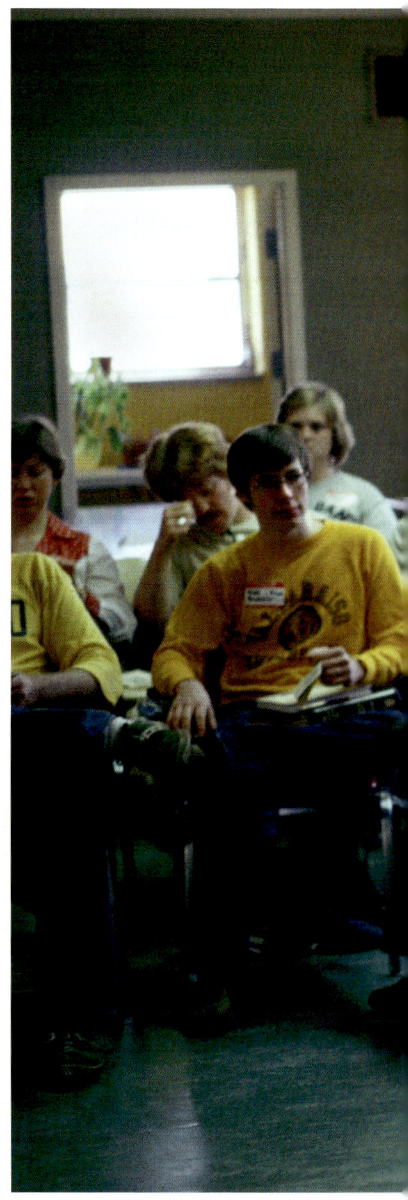

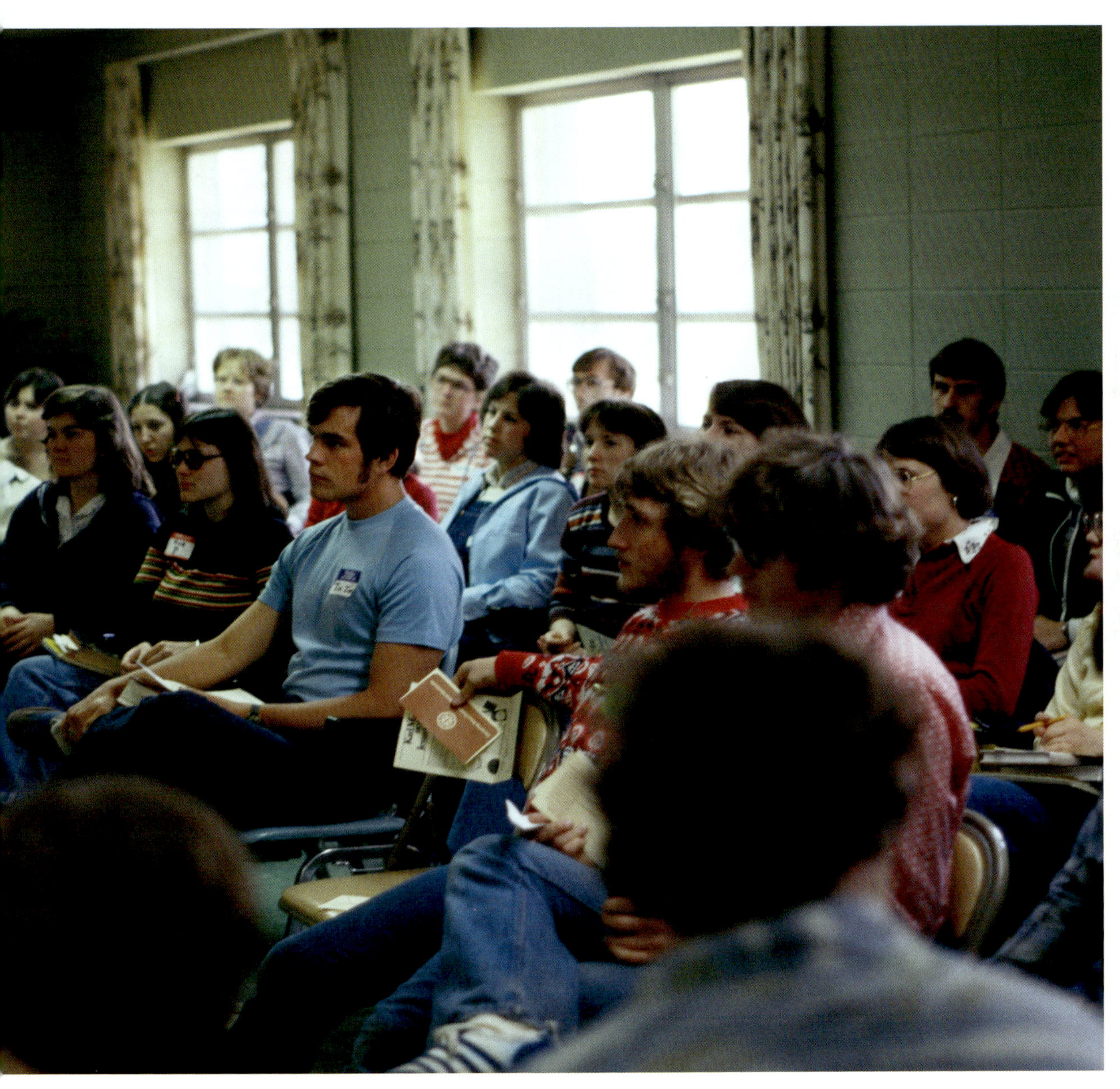

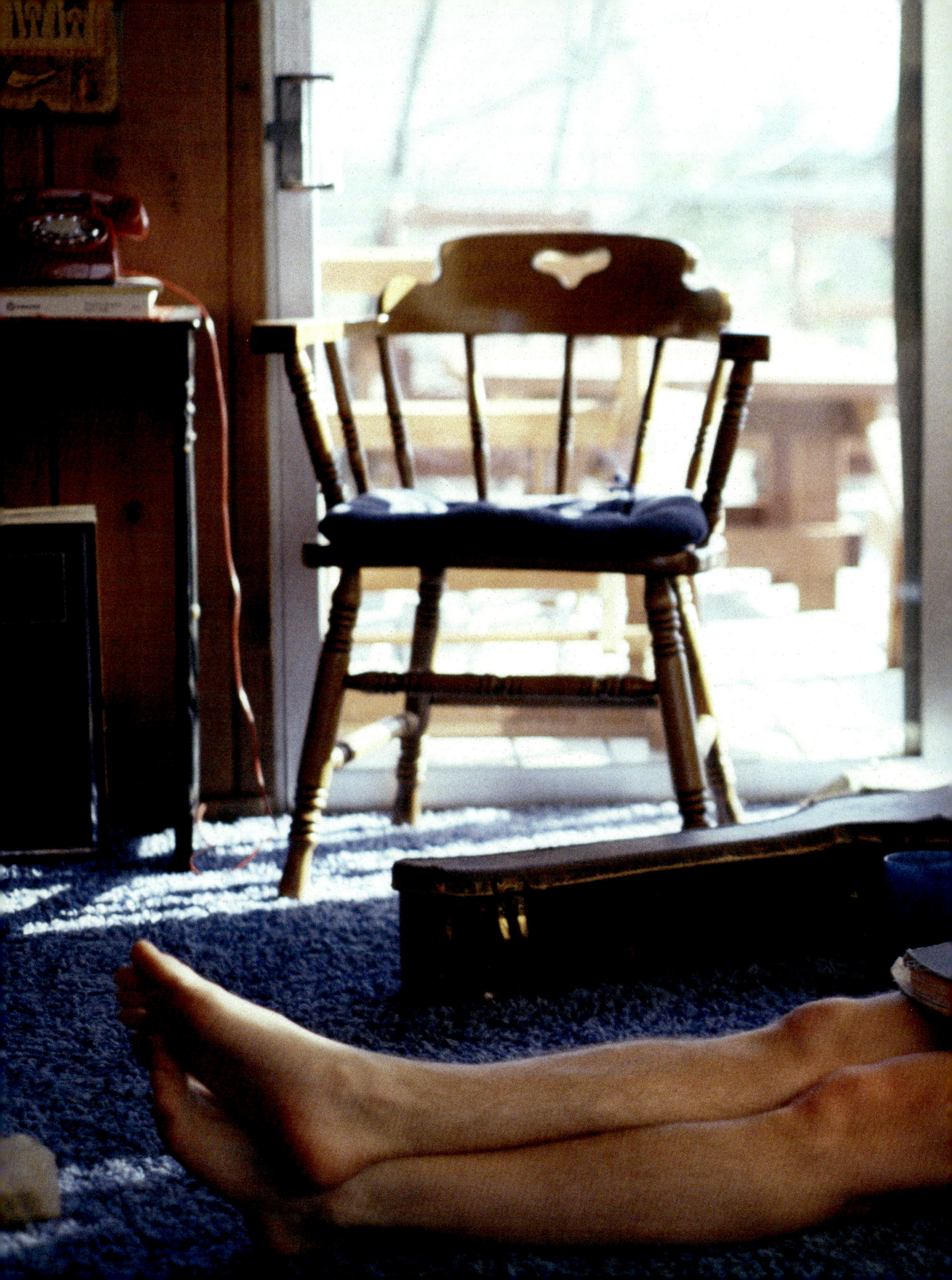

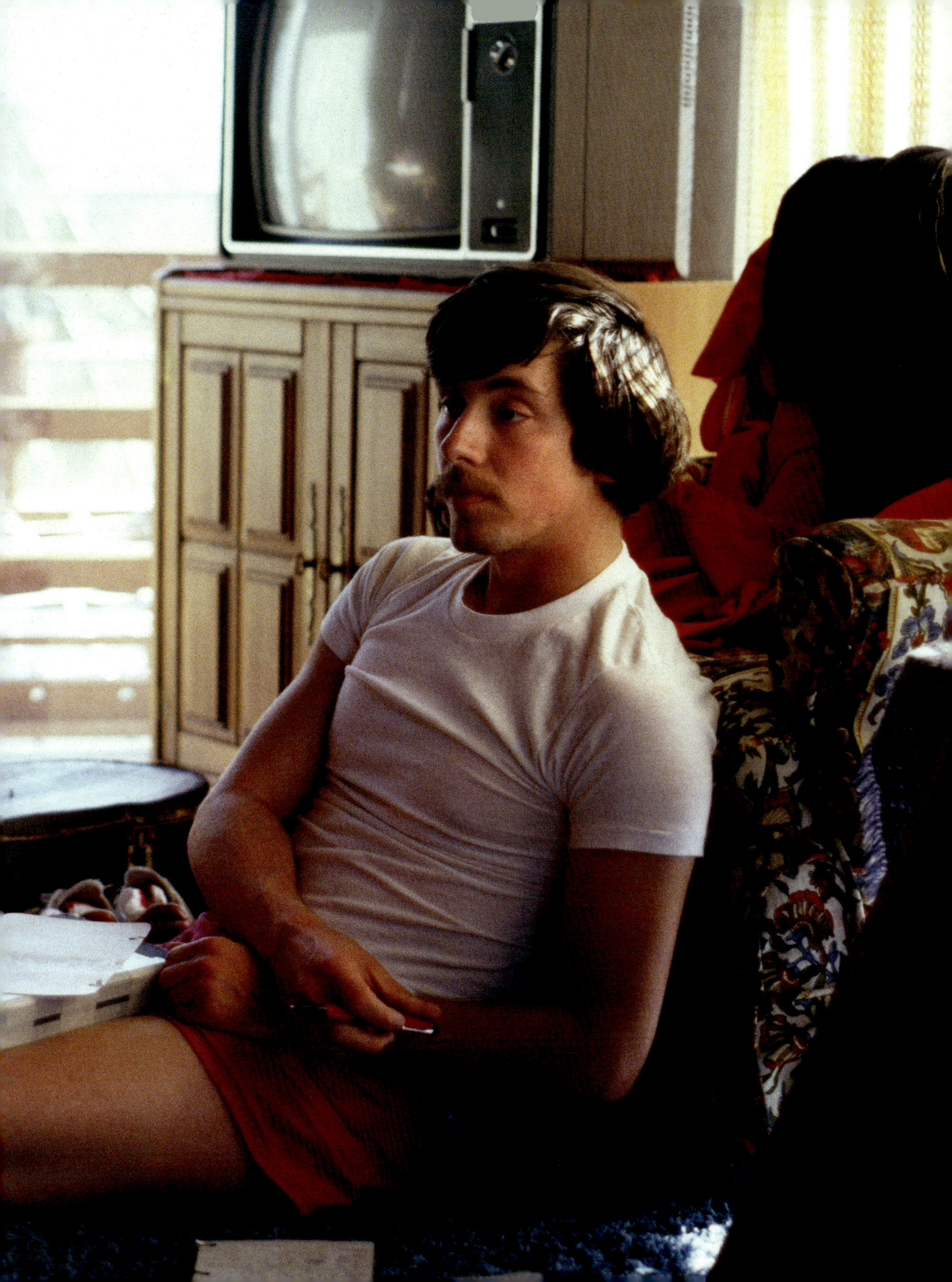

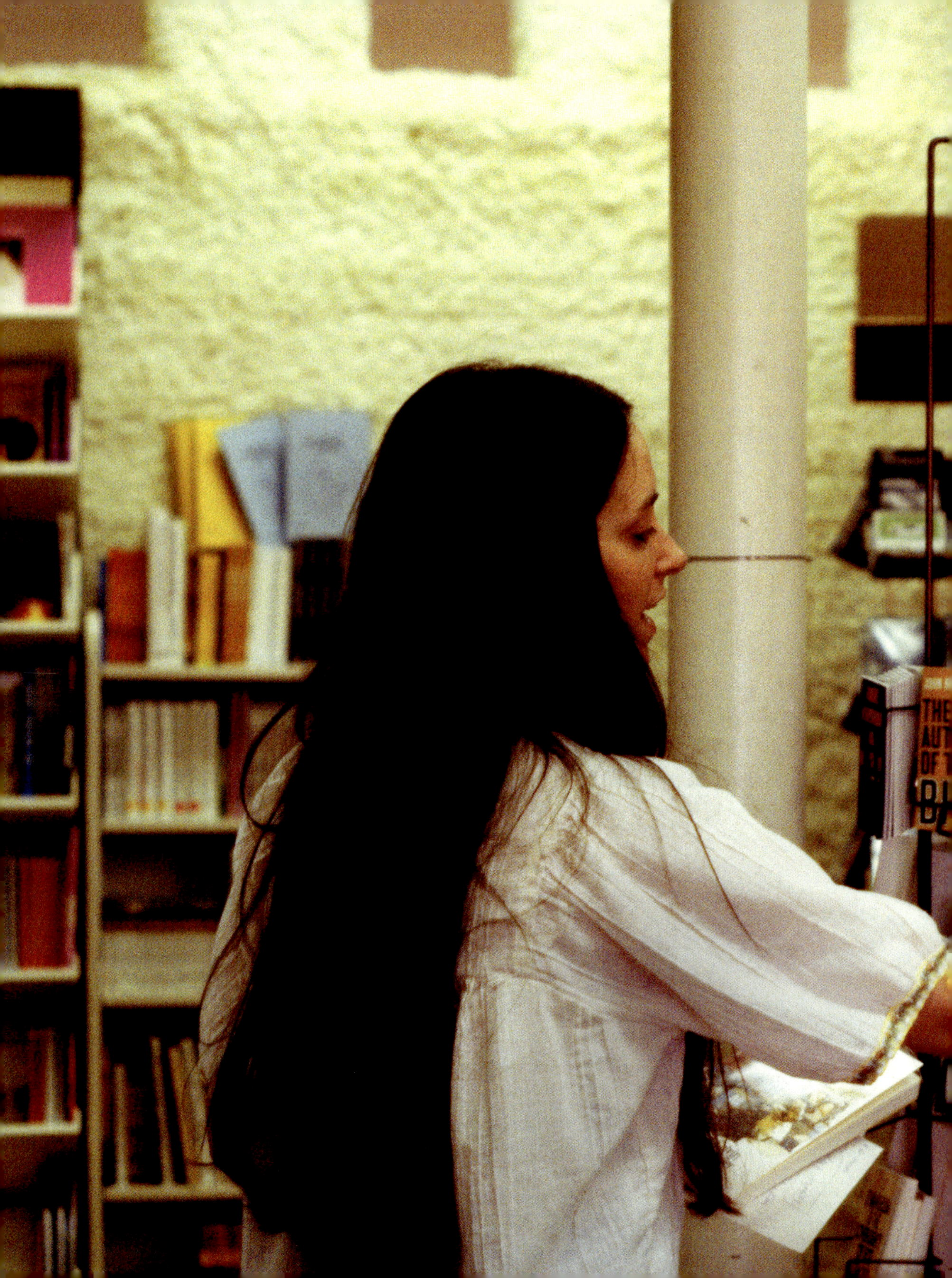

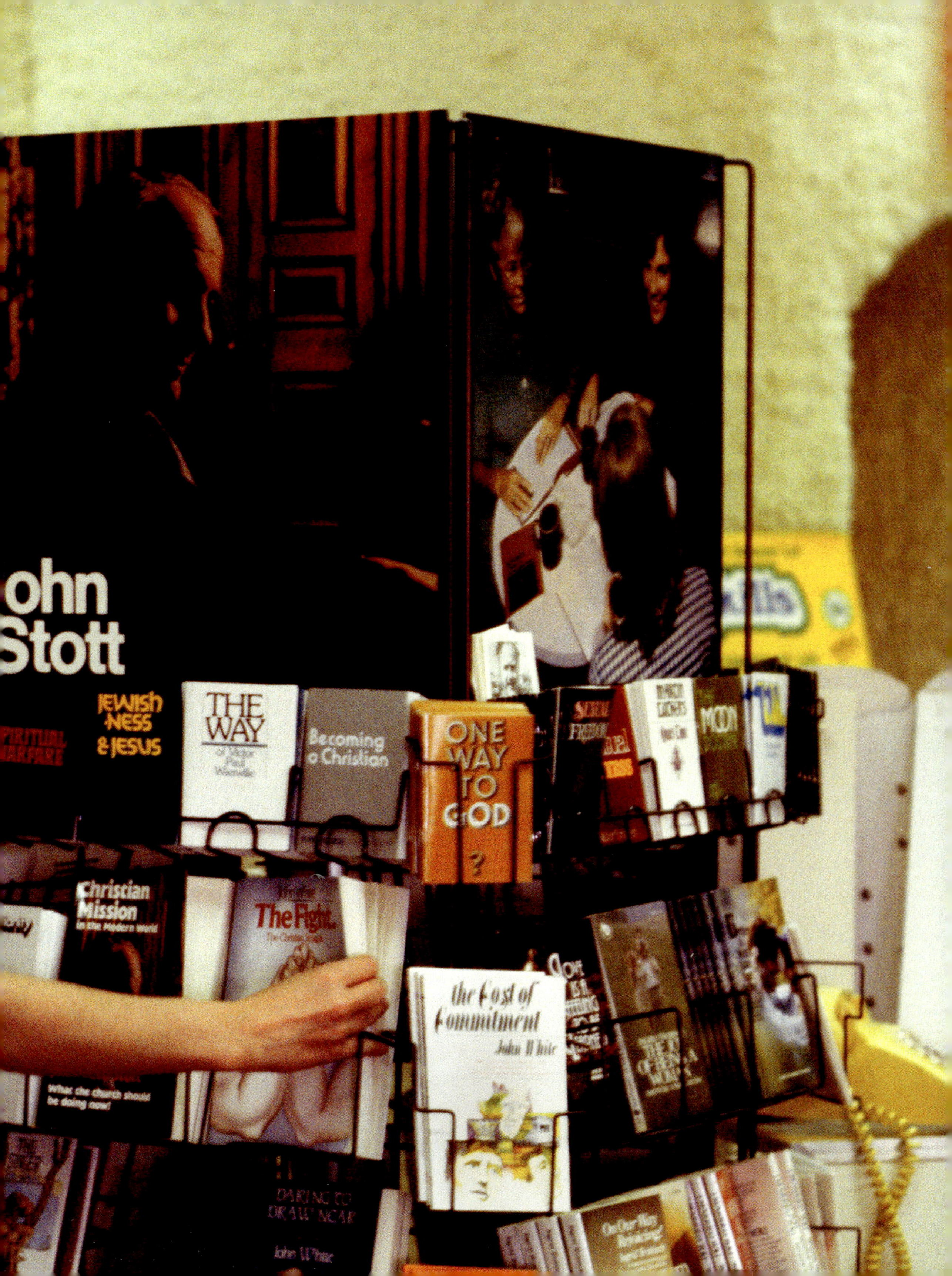
ohn
Stott
SPIRITUAL WARFARE
JEWISH-NESS & JESUS
THE WAY
of Victor Paul Wierwille
Becoming a Christian
ONE WAY TO GOD ?
SOCIAL Freedom
MOON
Christian Mission in the Modern World
The Fight.
the Cost of Commitment
John White
What the church should be doing now!
DARING TO DRAW NEAR
John White

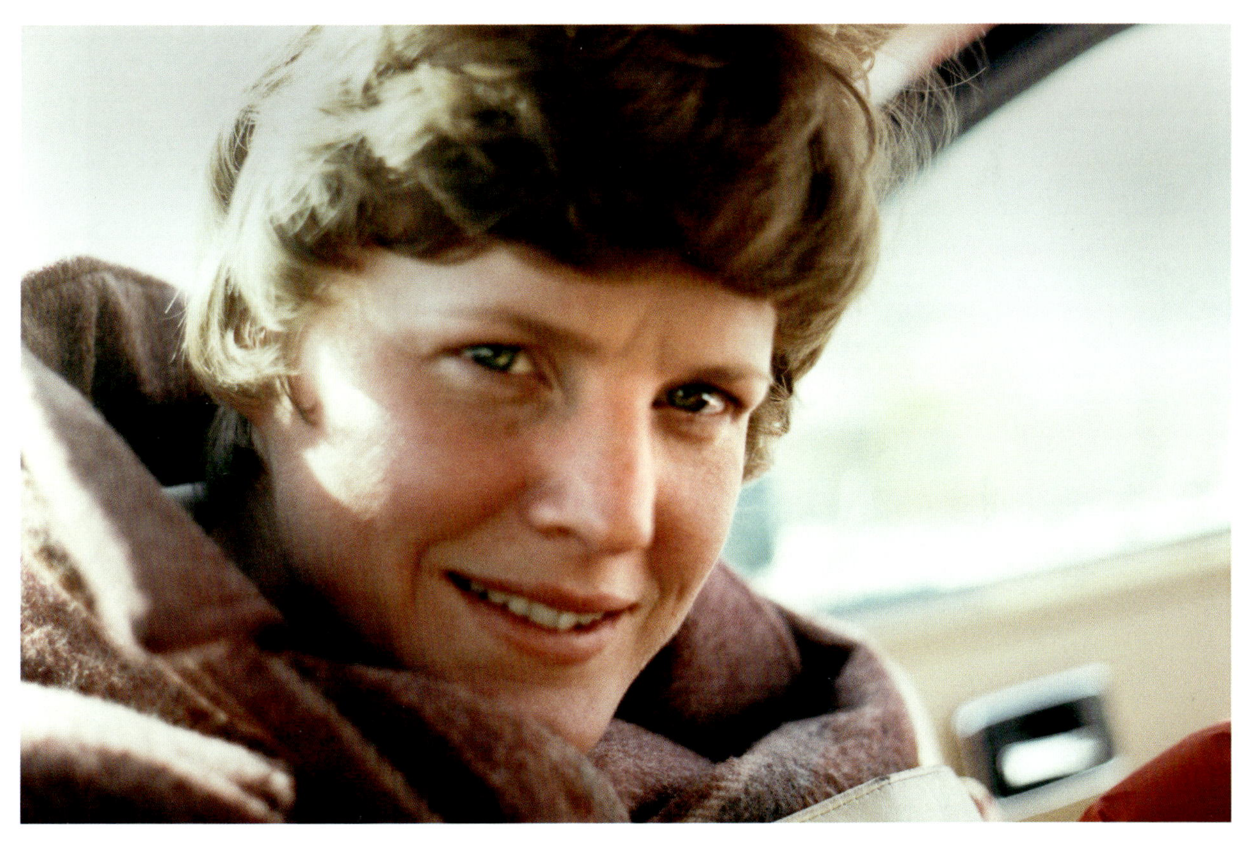

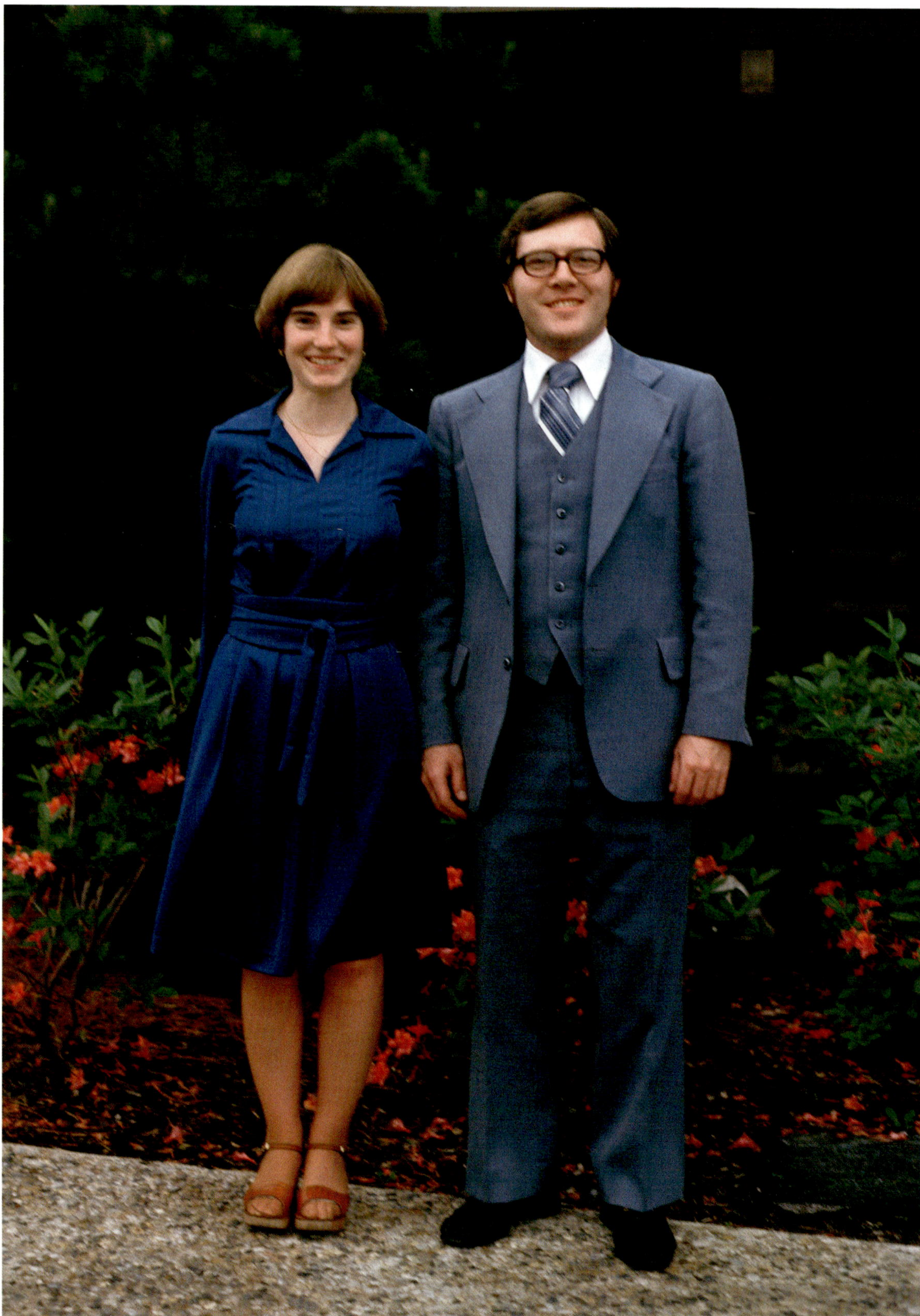

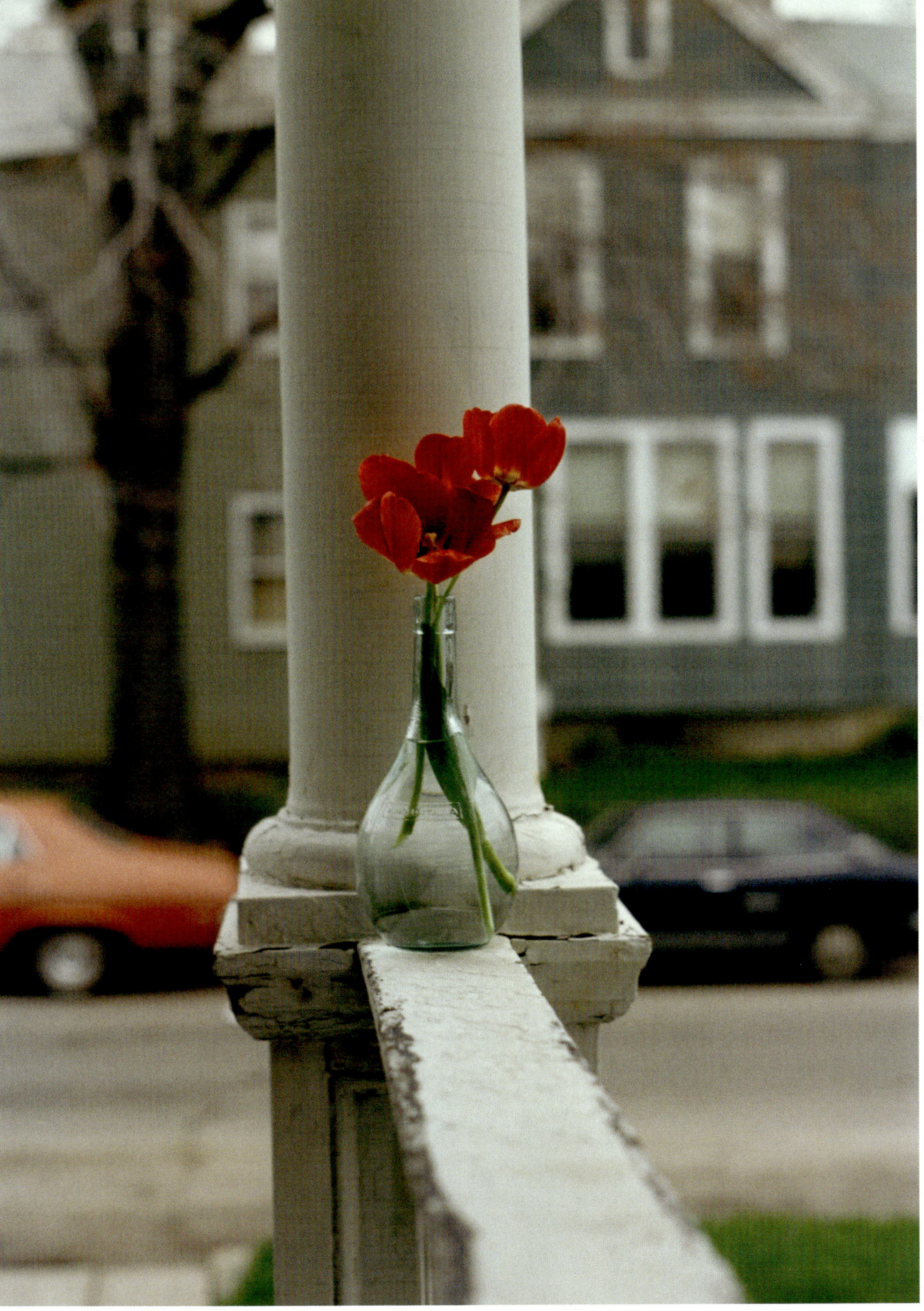

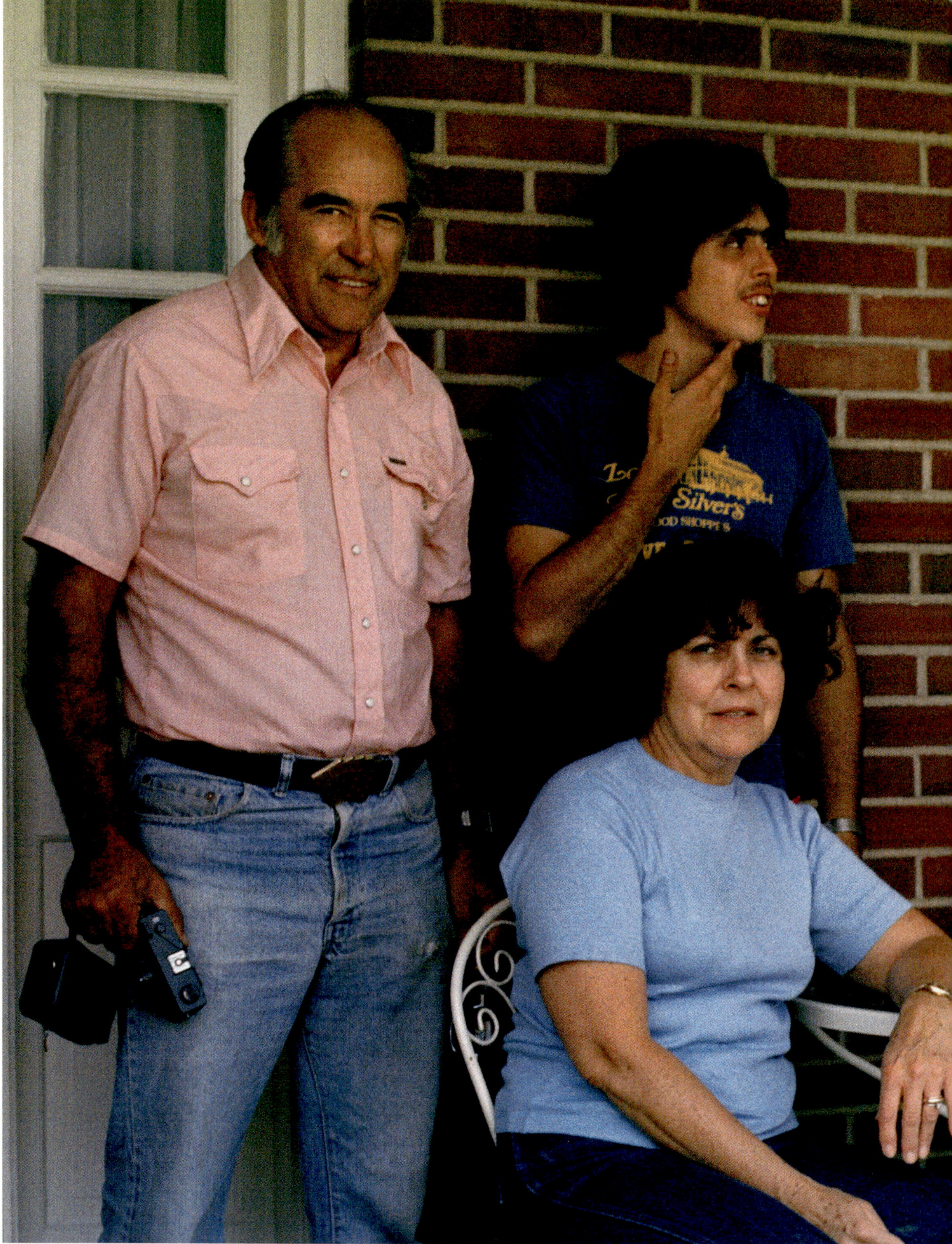
Silver's
OOD SHOPPE'S

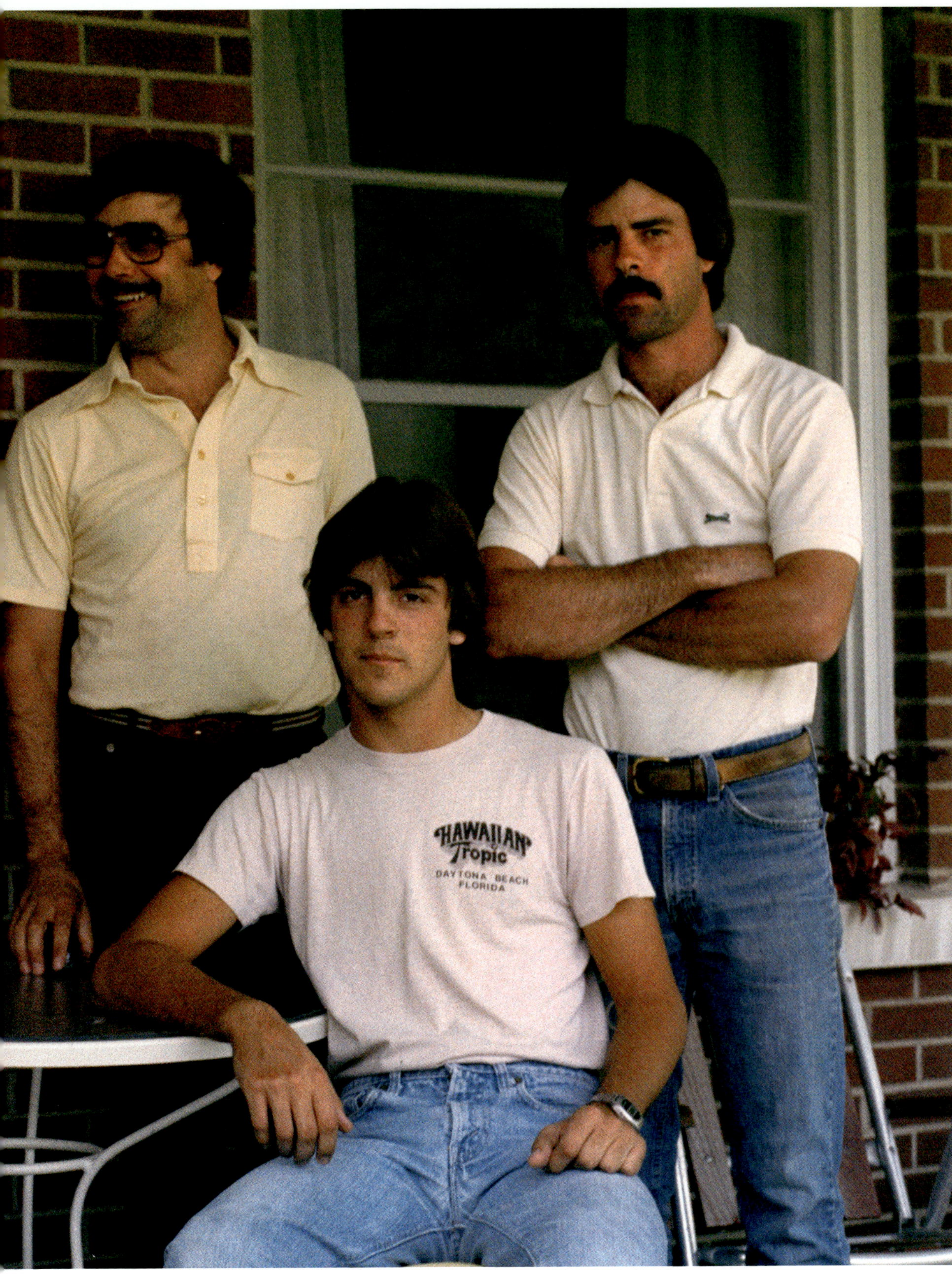

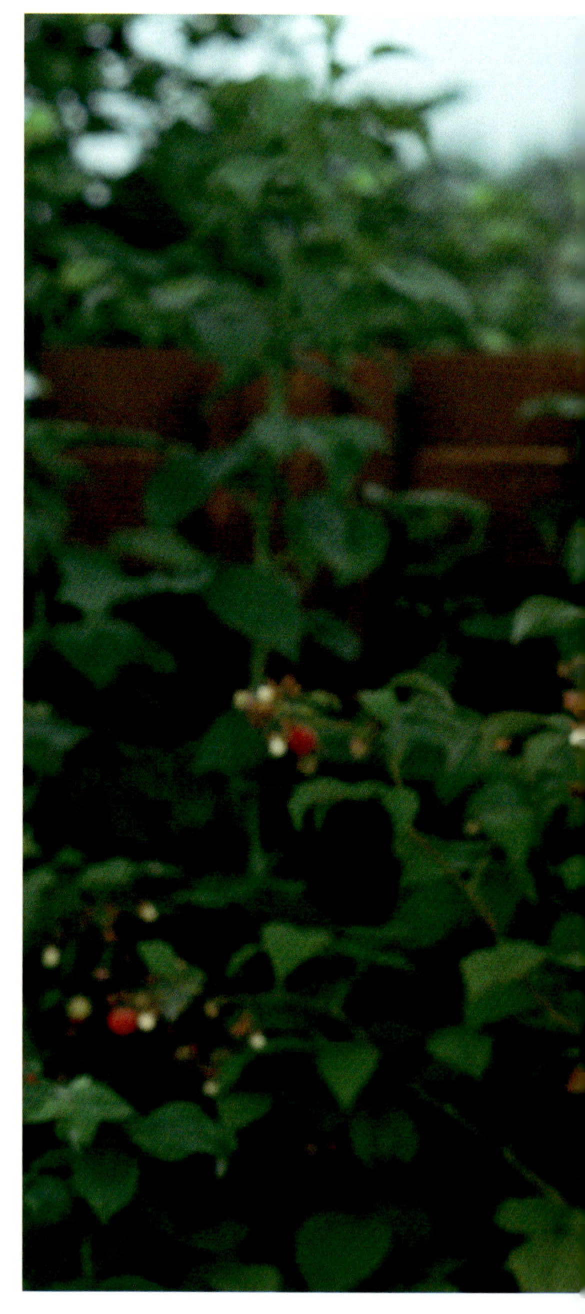

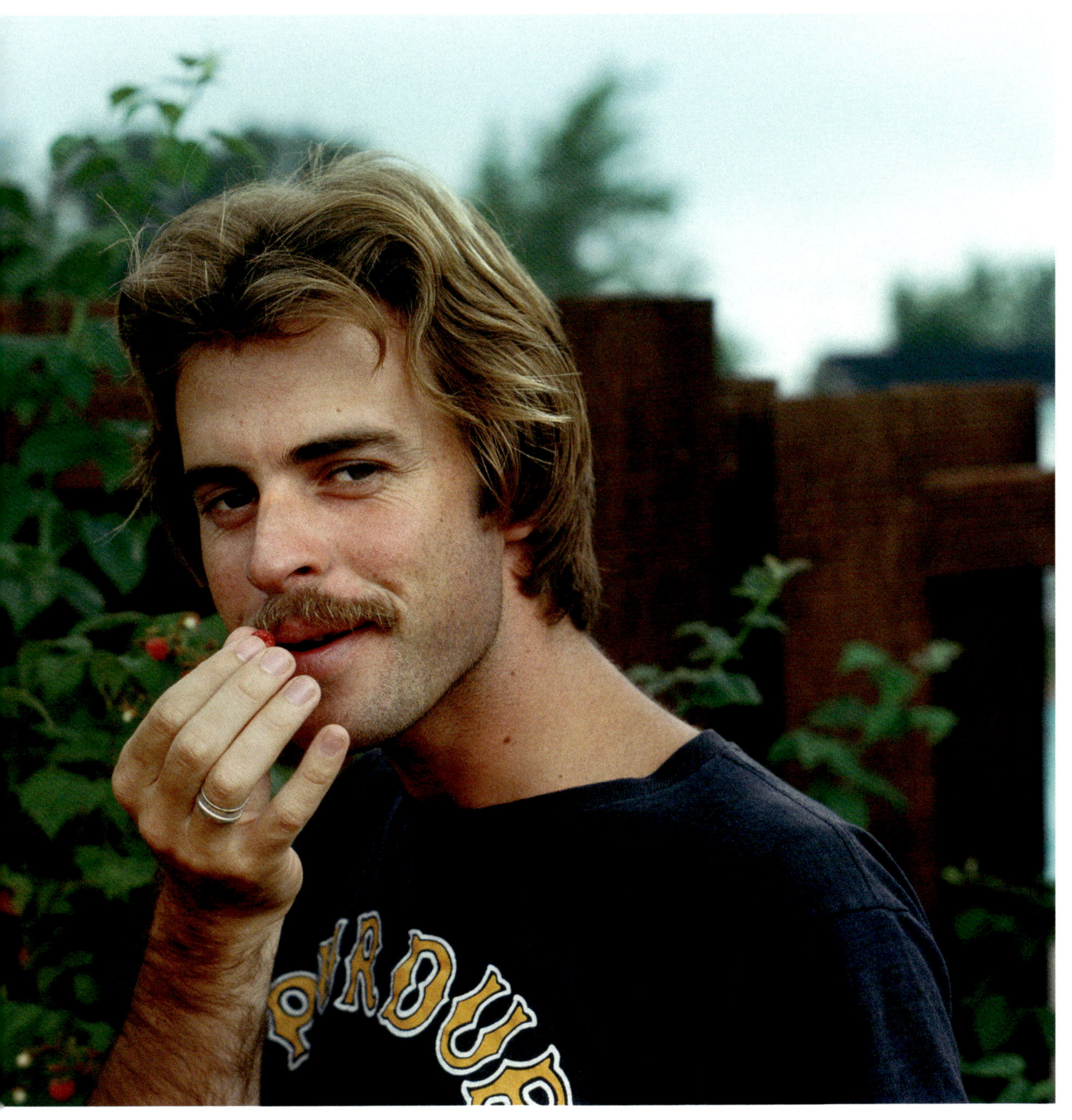

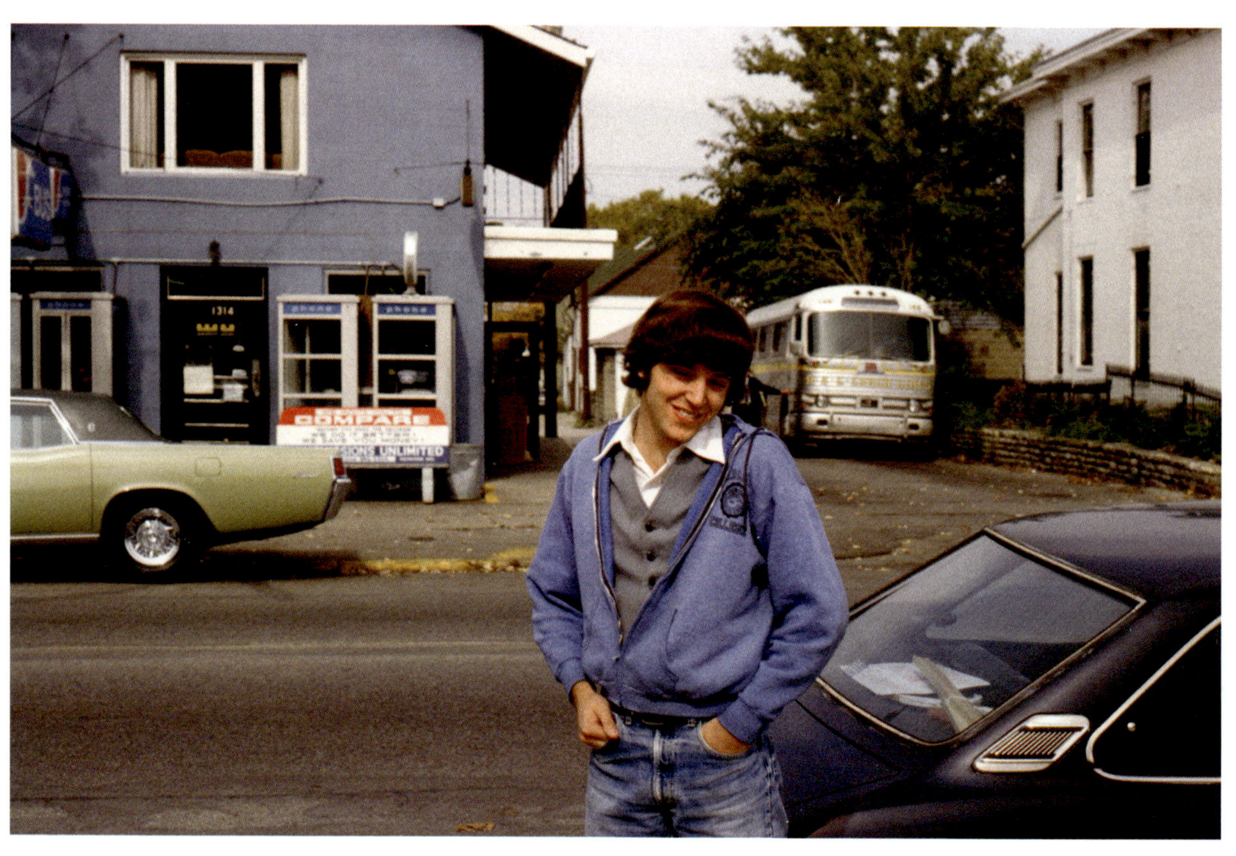

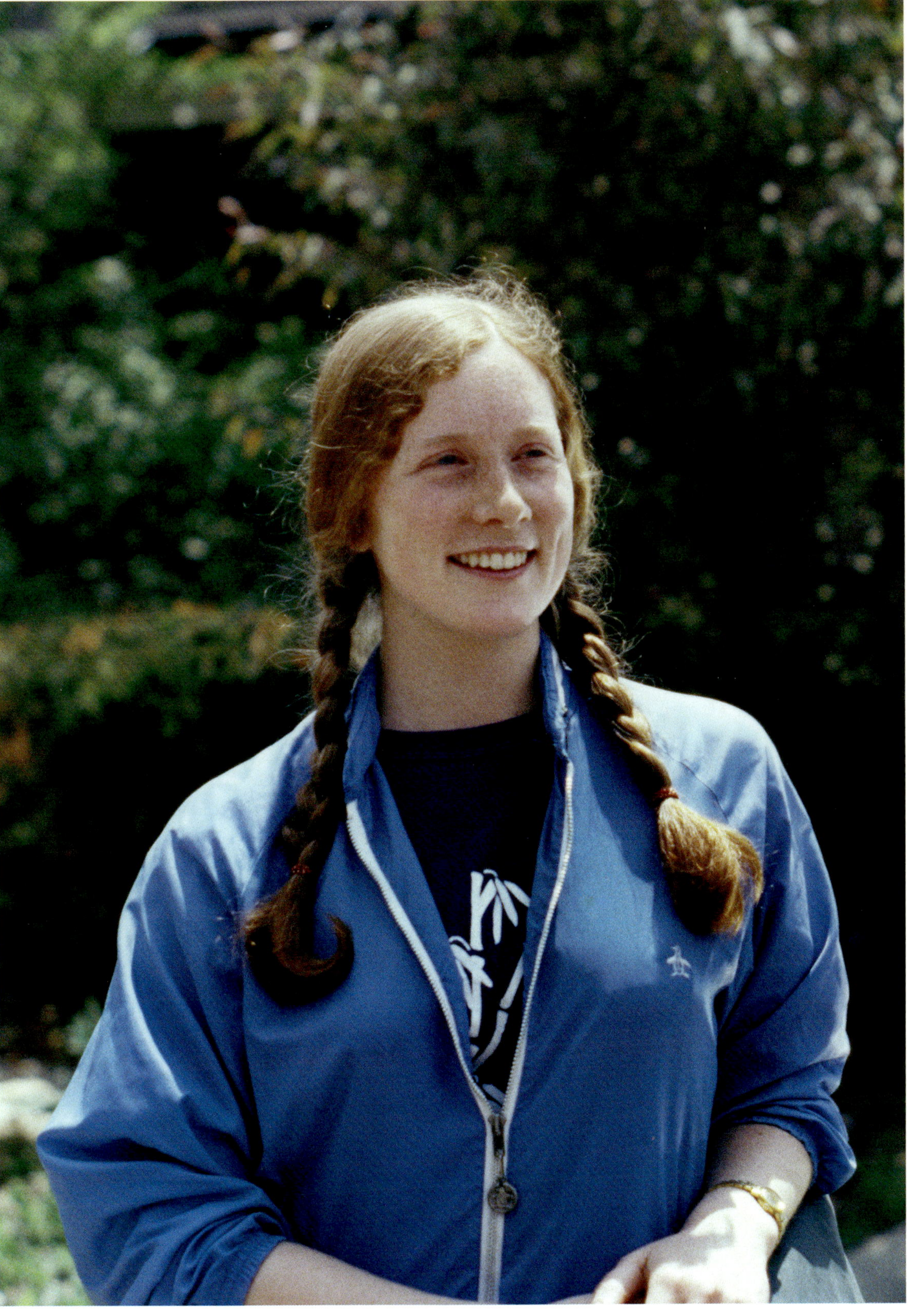

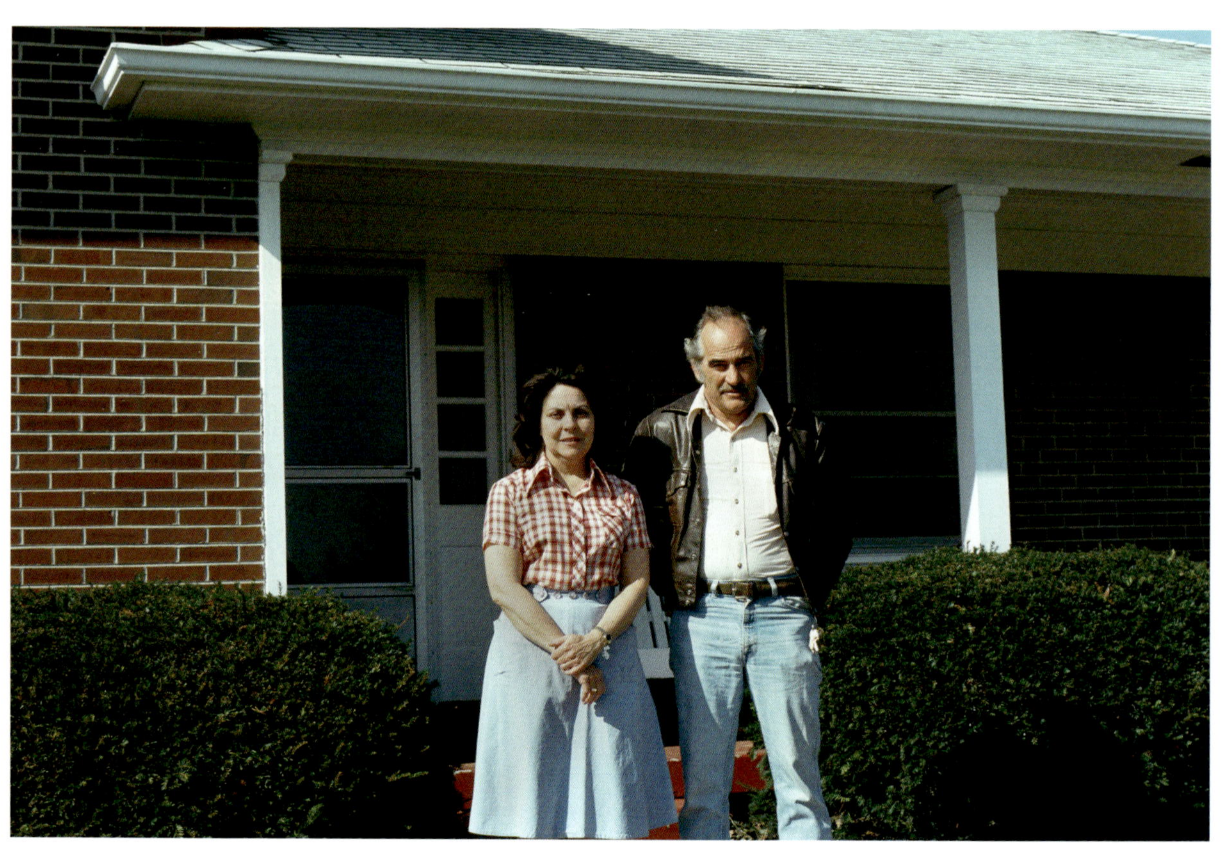

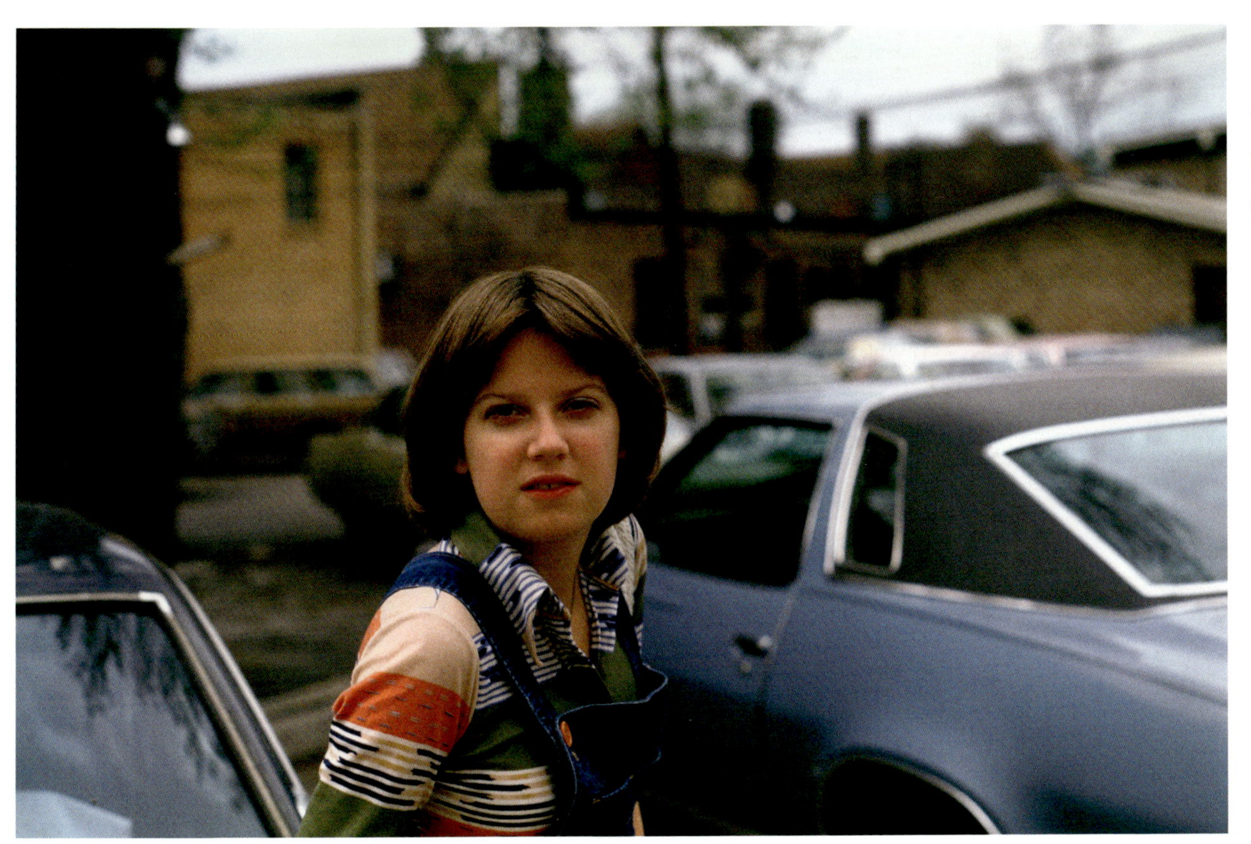

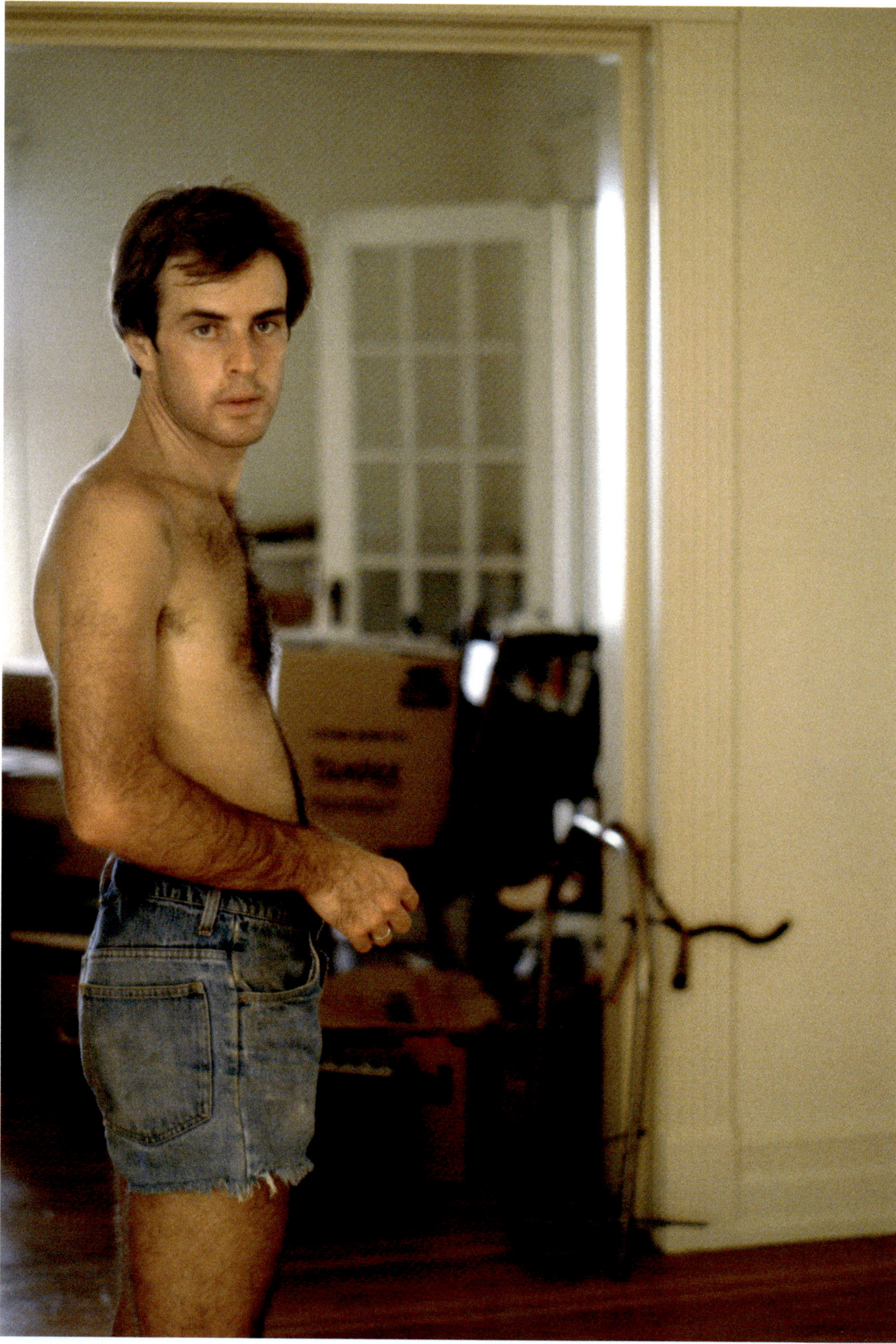

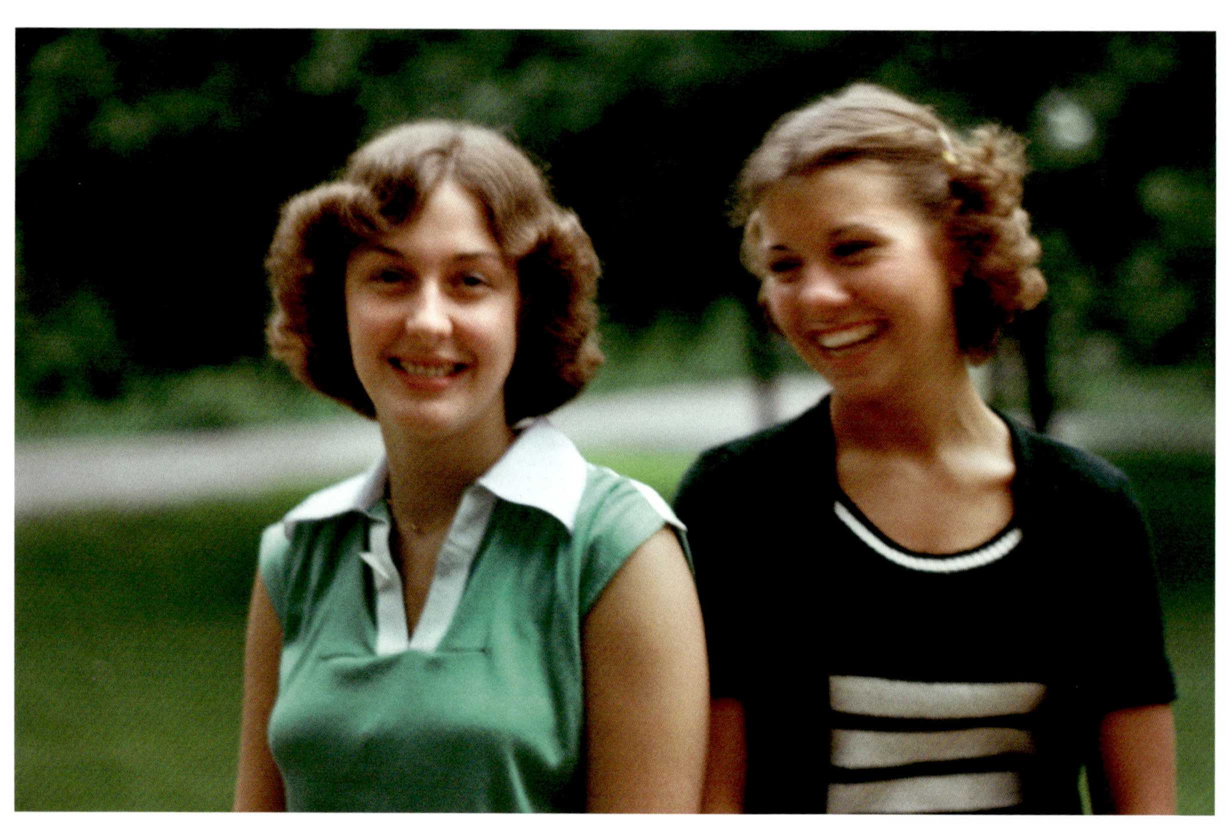

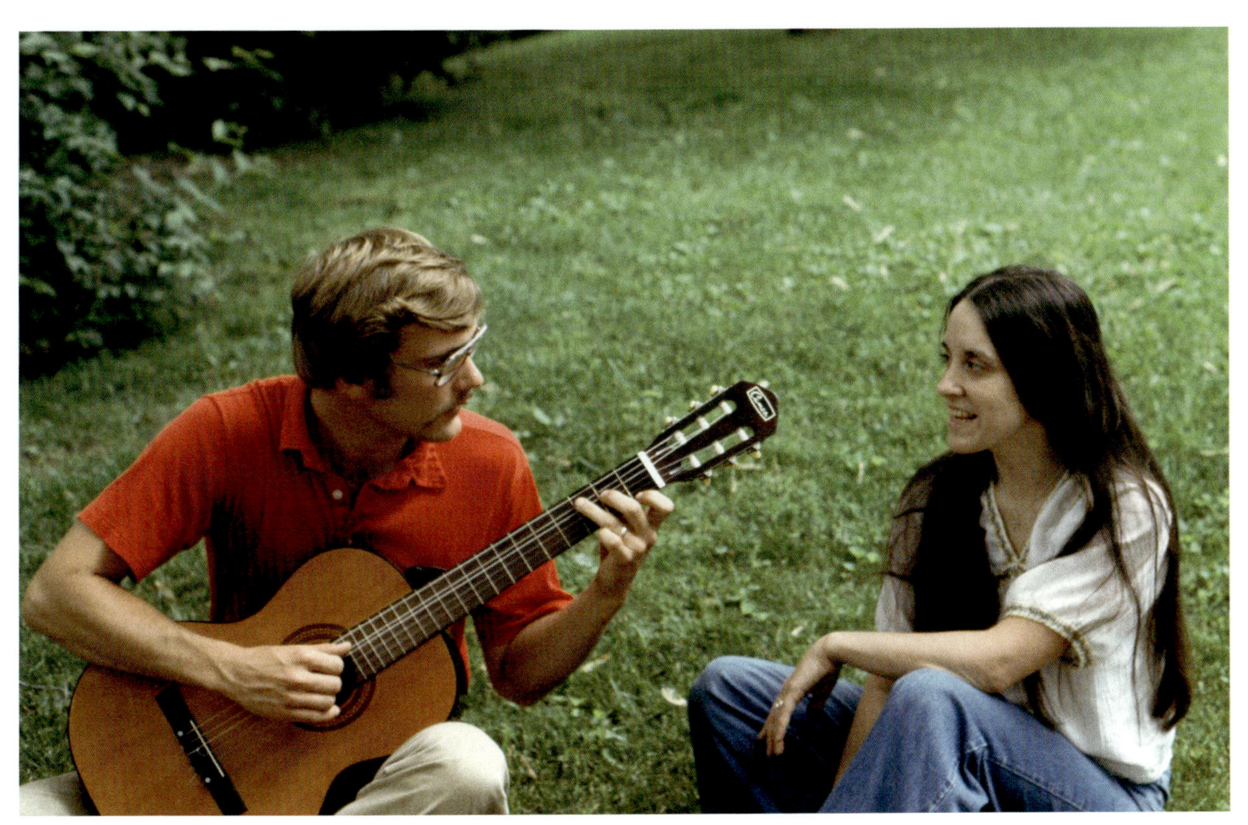

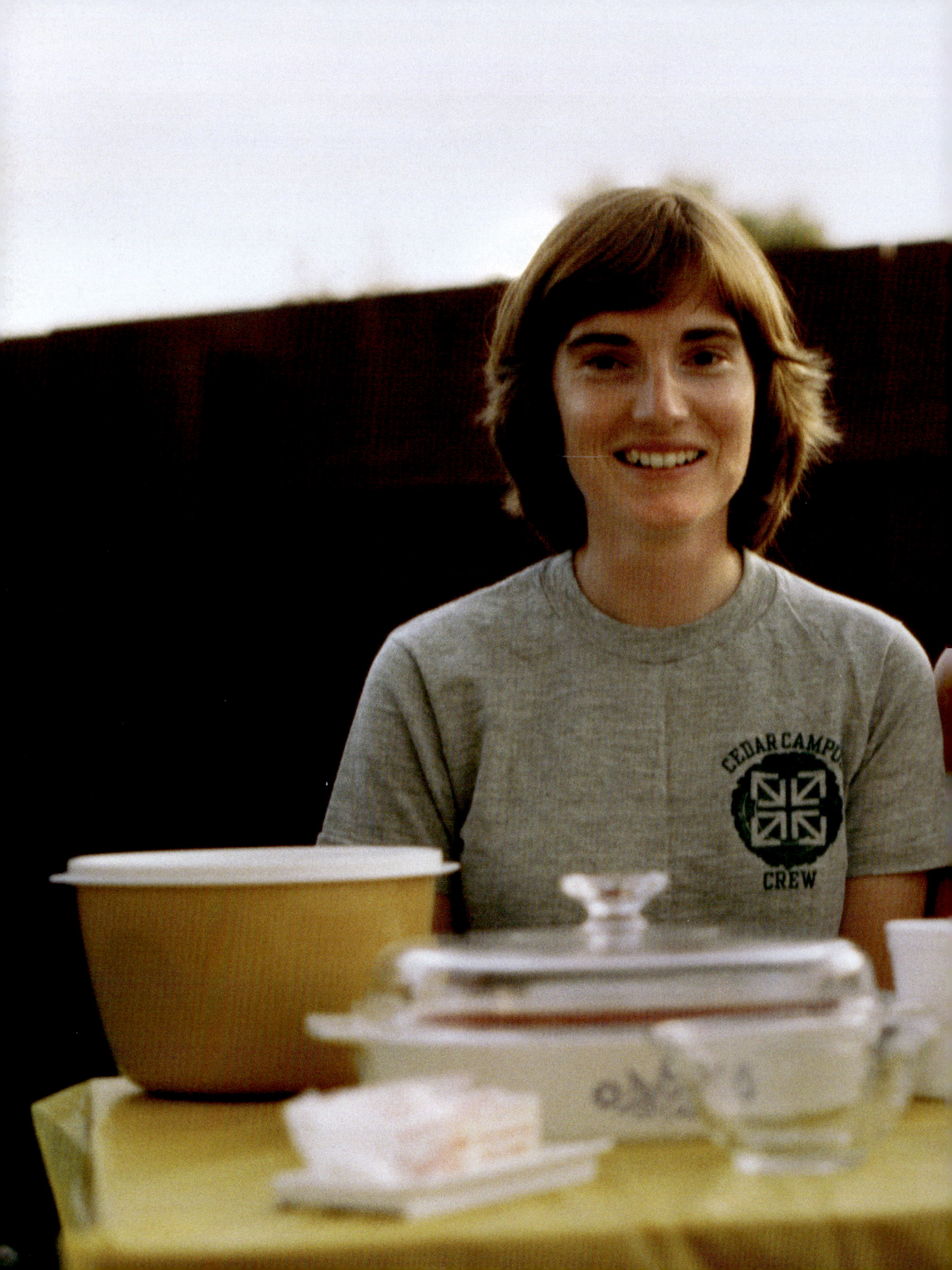
CEDAR CAMPUS
CREW

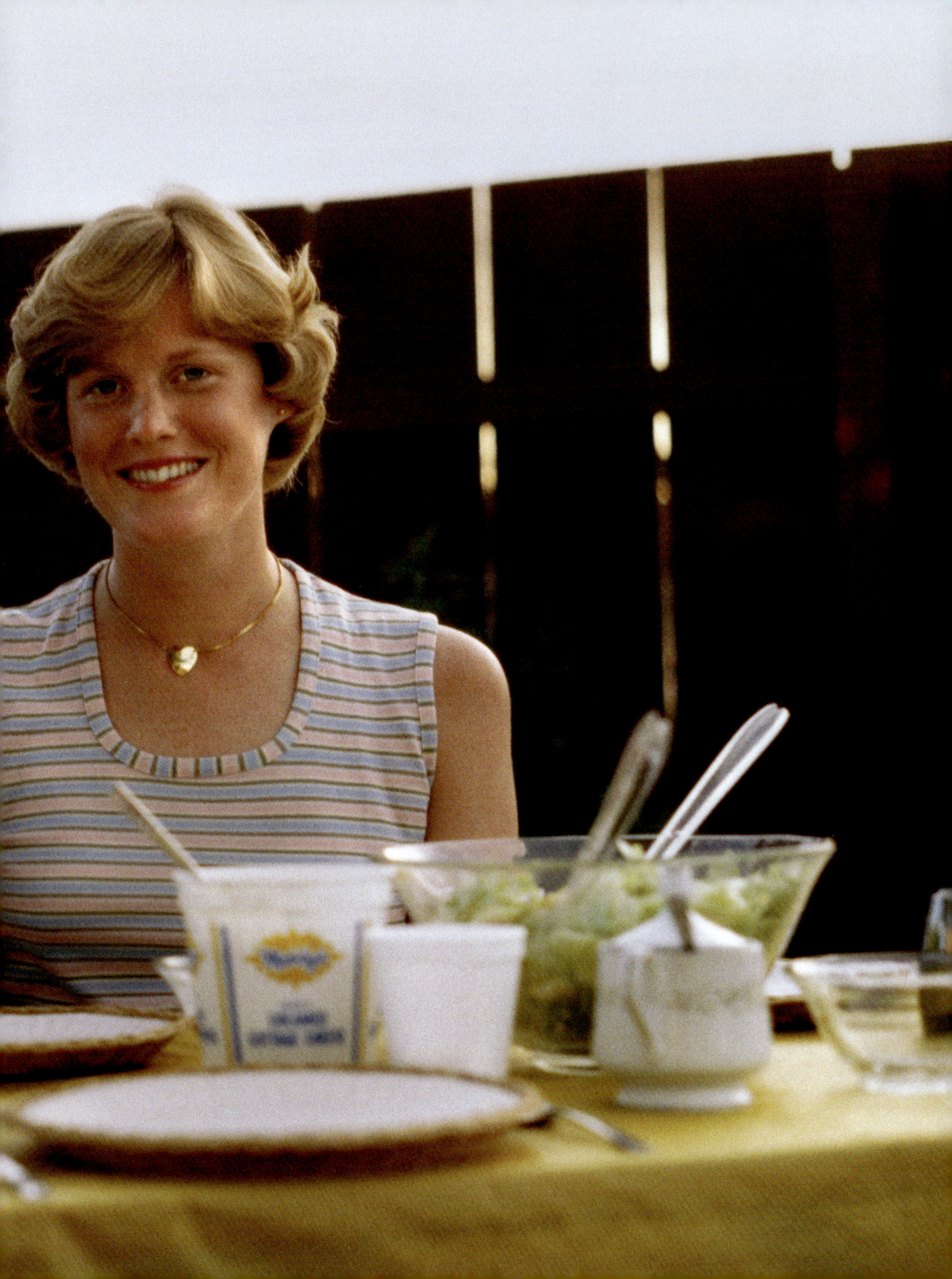

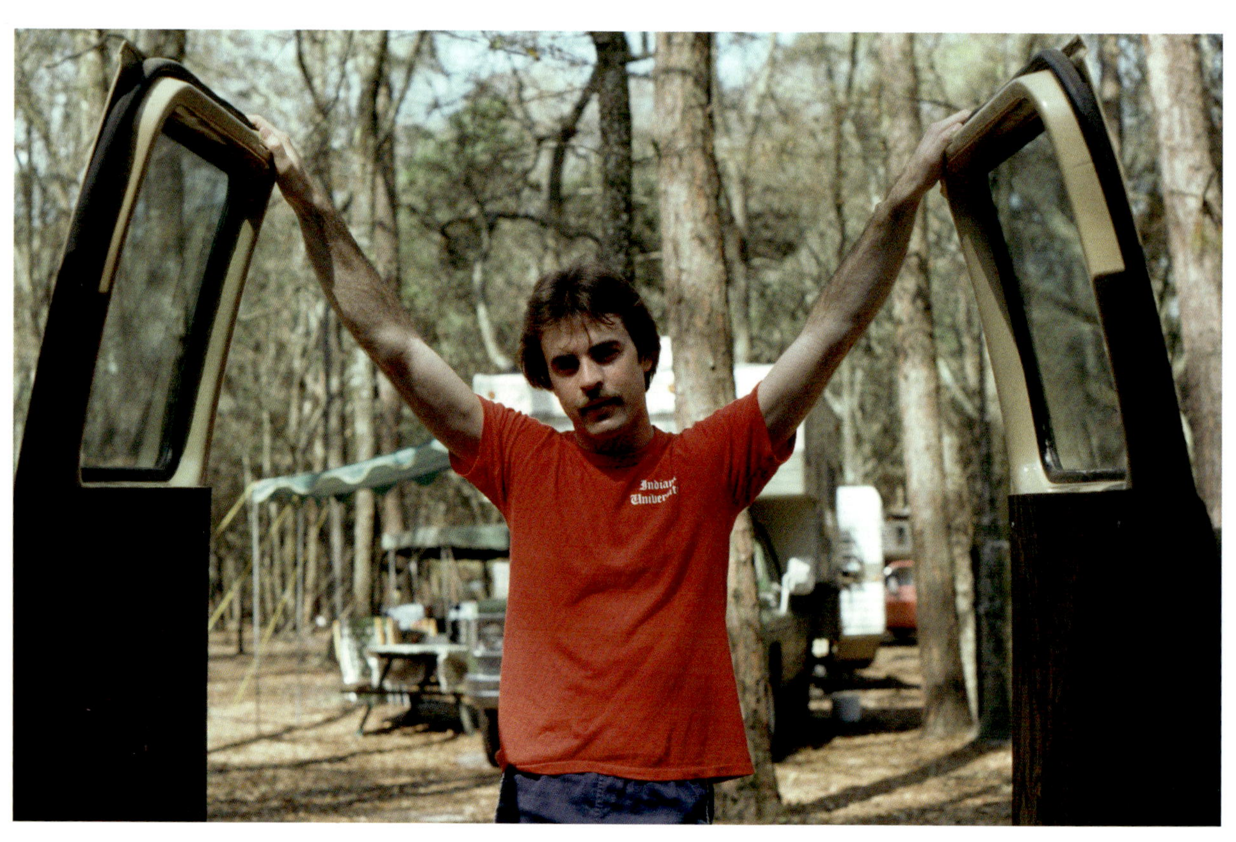

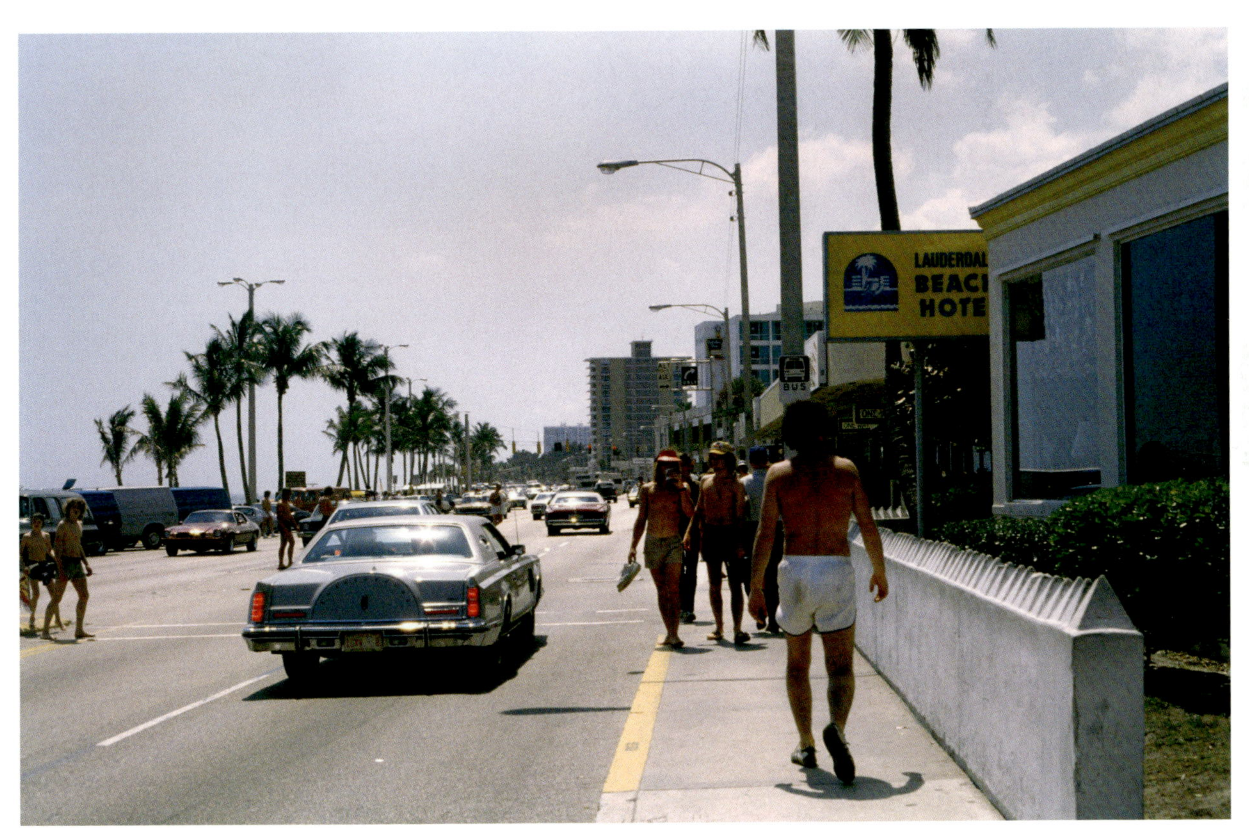
LAUDERDALE
BEACH
HOTEL
ALT
A1A
BUS

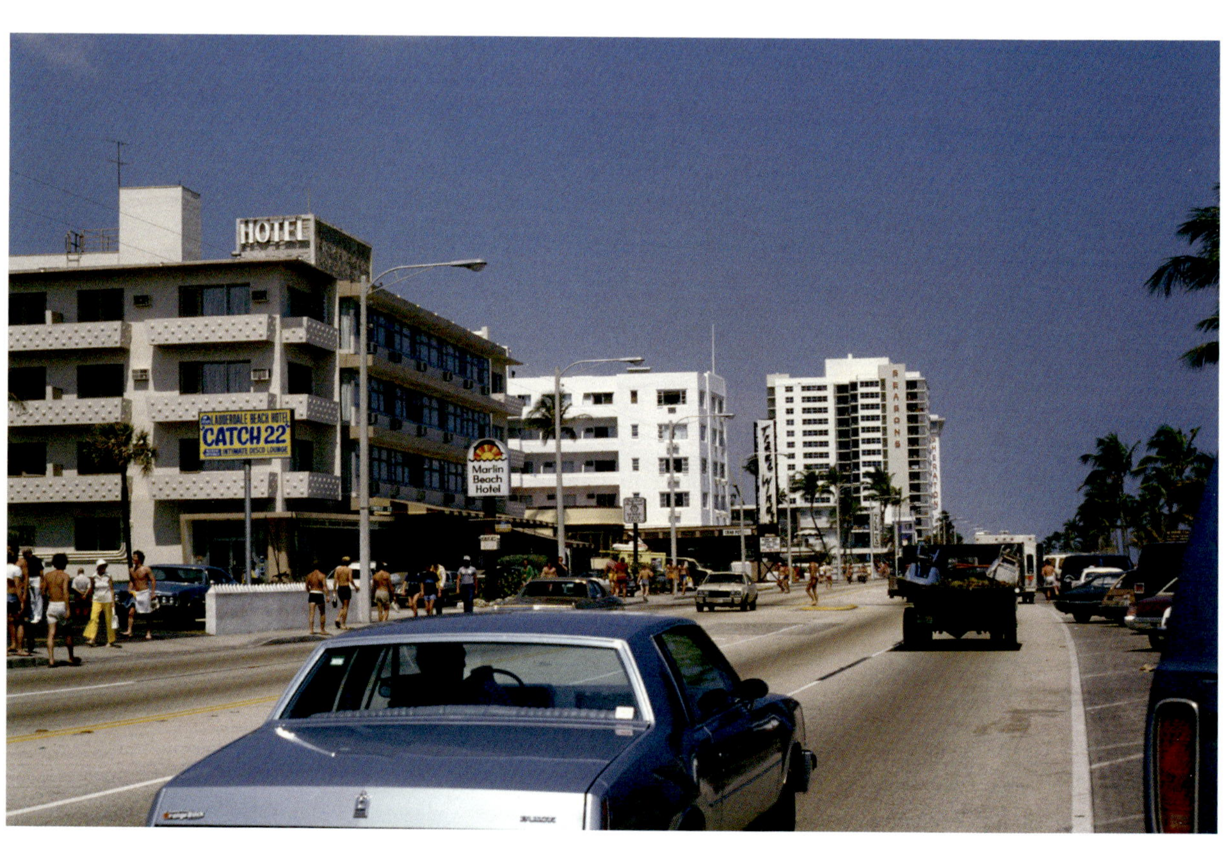
HOTEL
LAUDERDALE BEACH HOTEL
CATCH 22
INTIMATE DISCO LOUNGE
Marlin
Beach
Hotel
FREE WAY

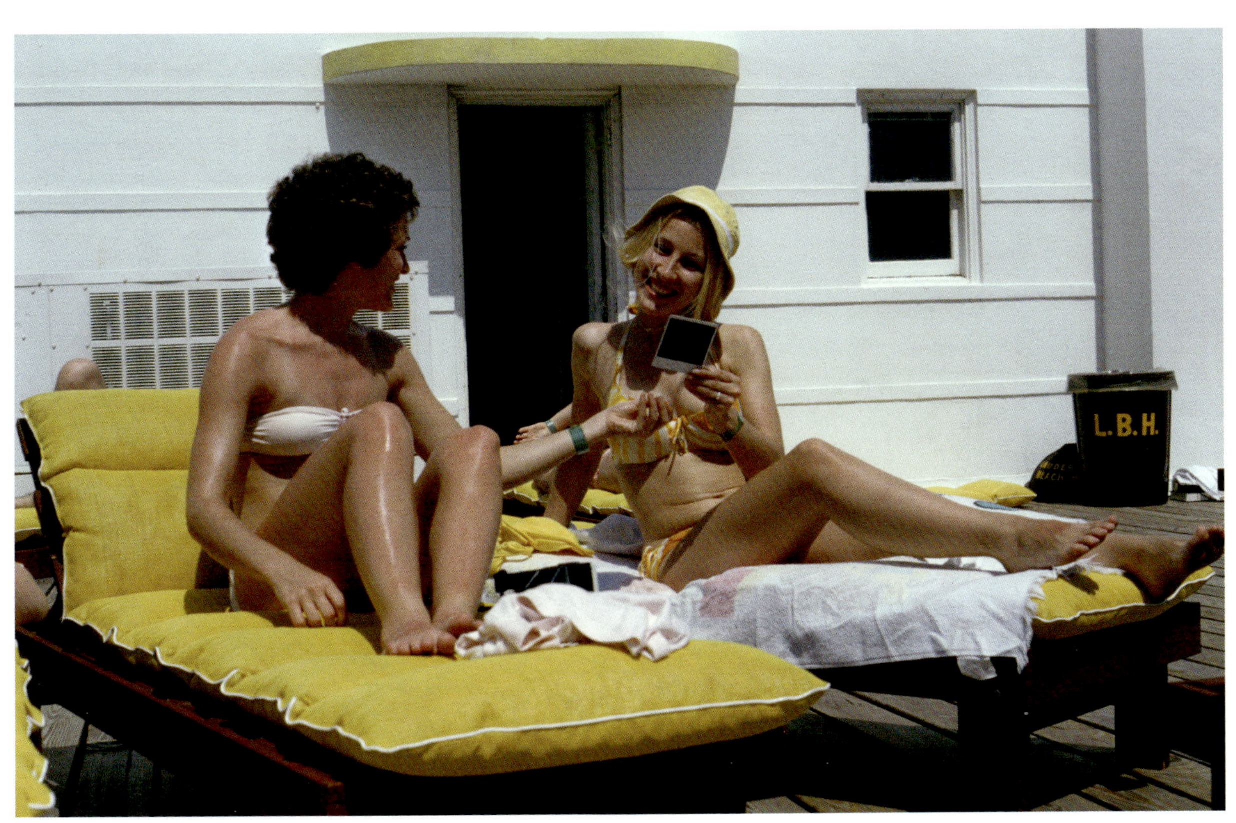

L.B.H.

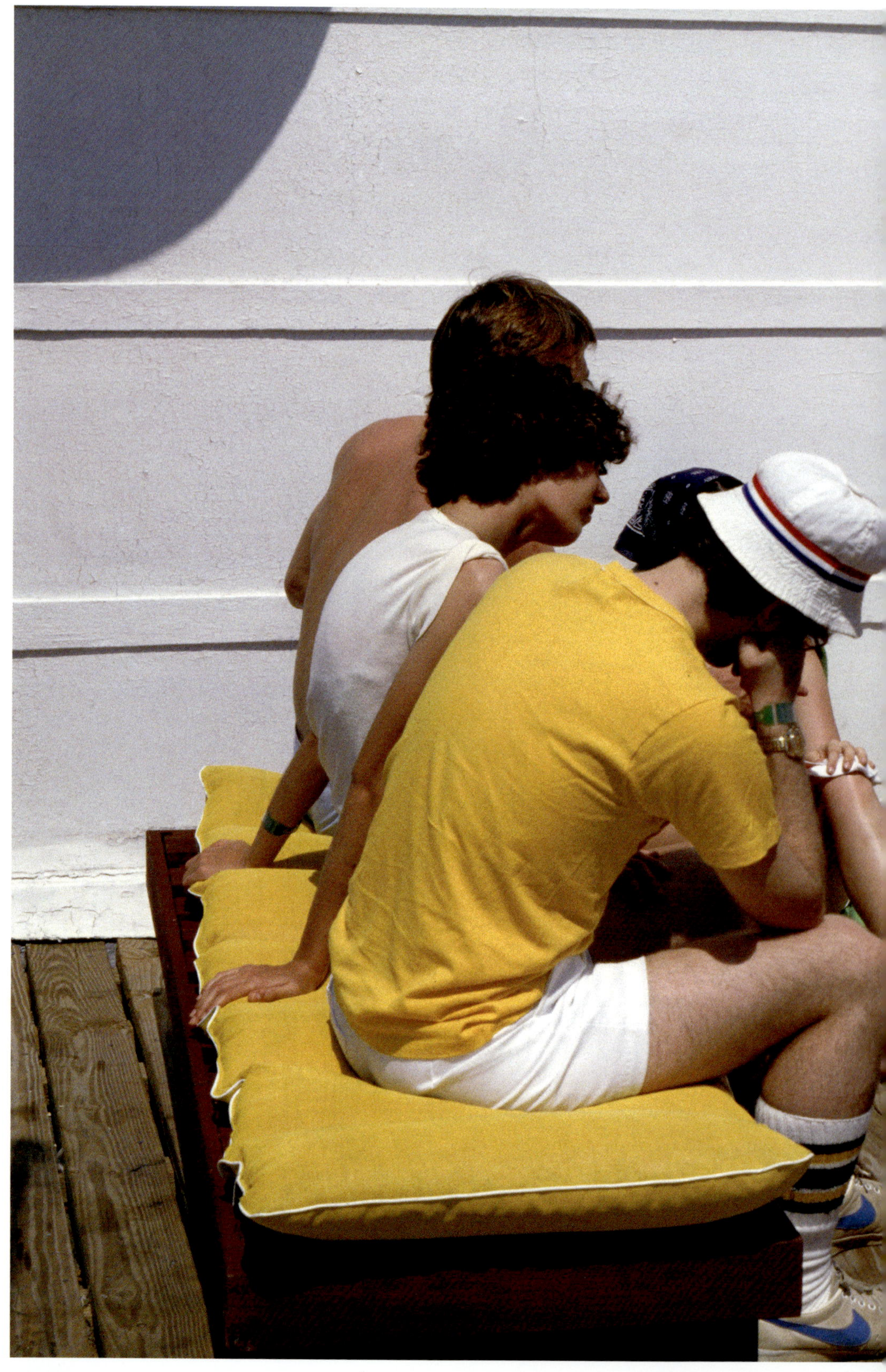

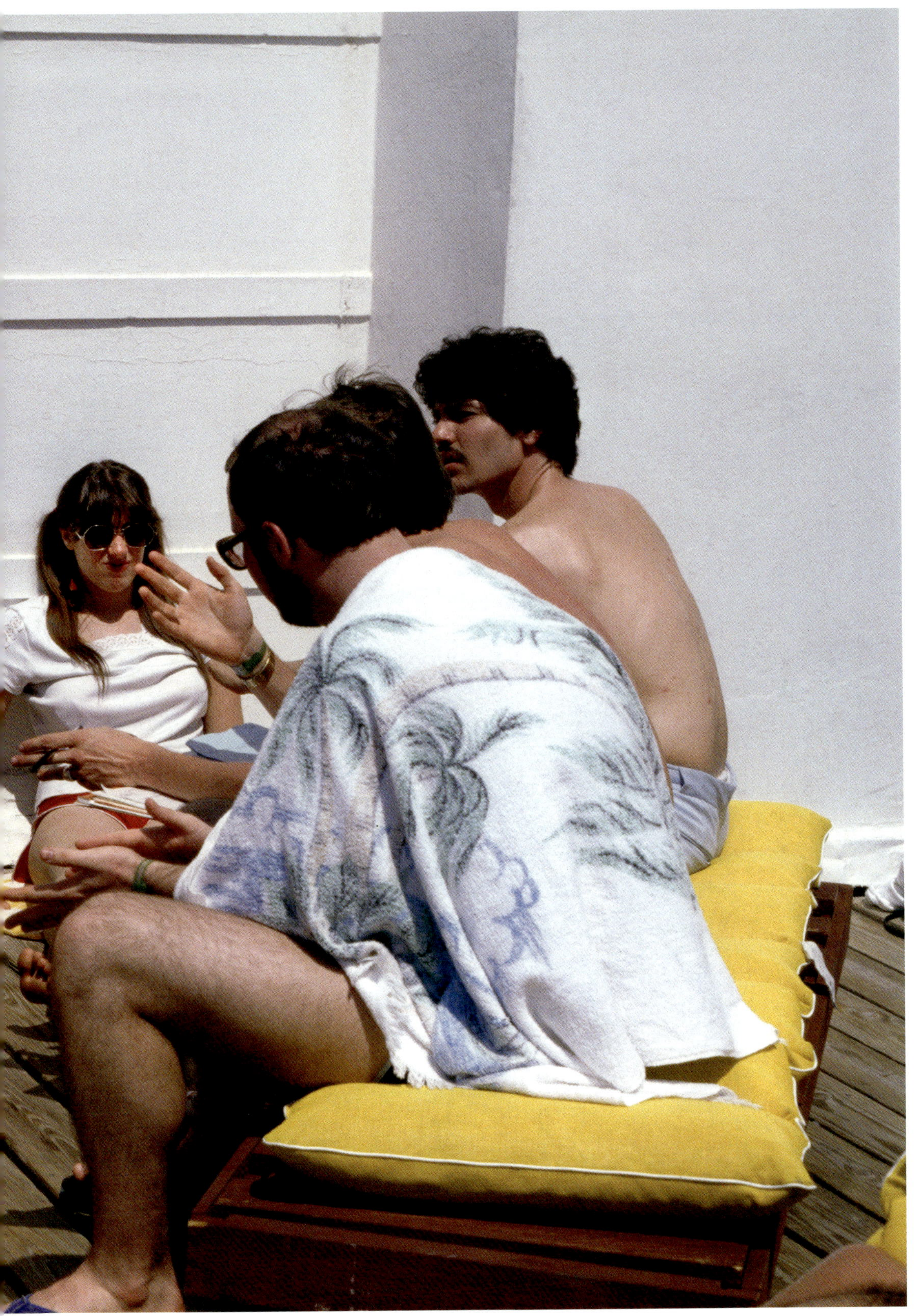

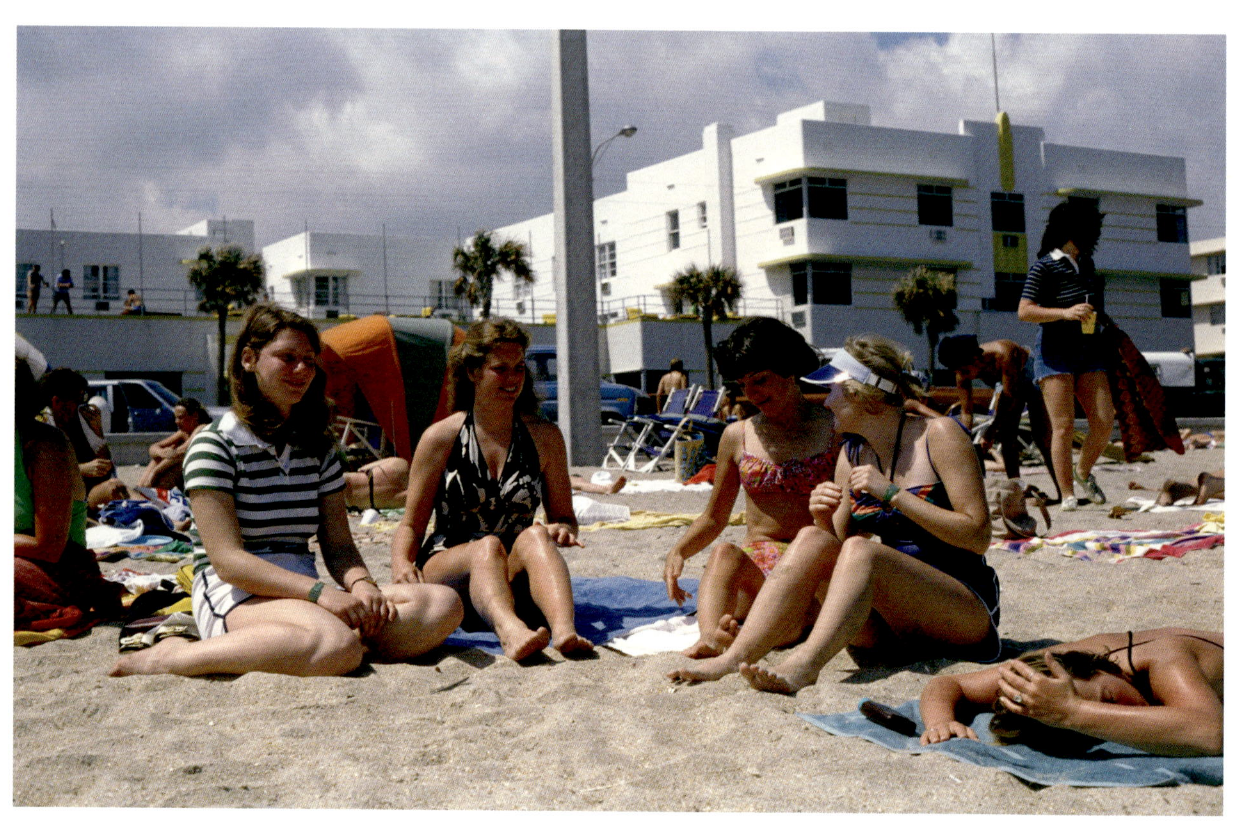

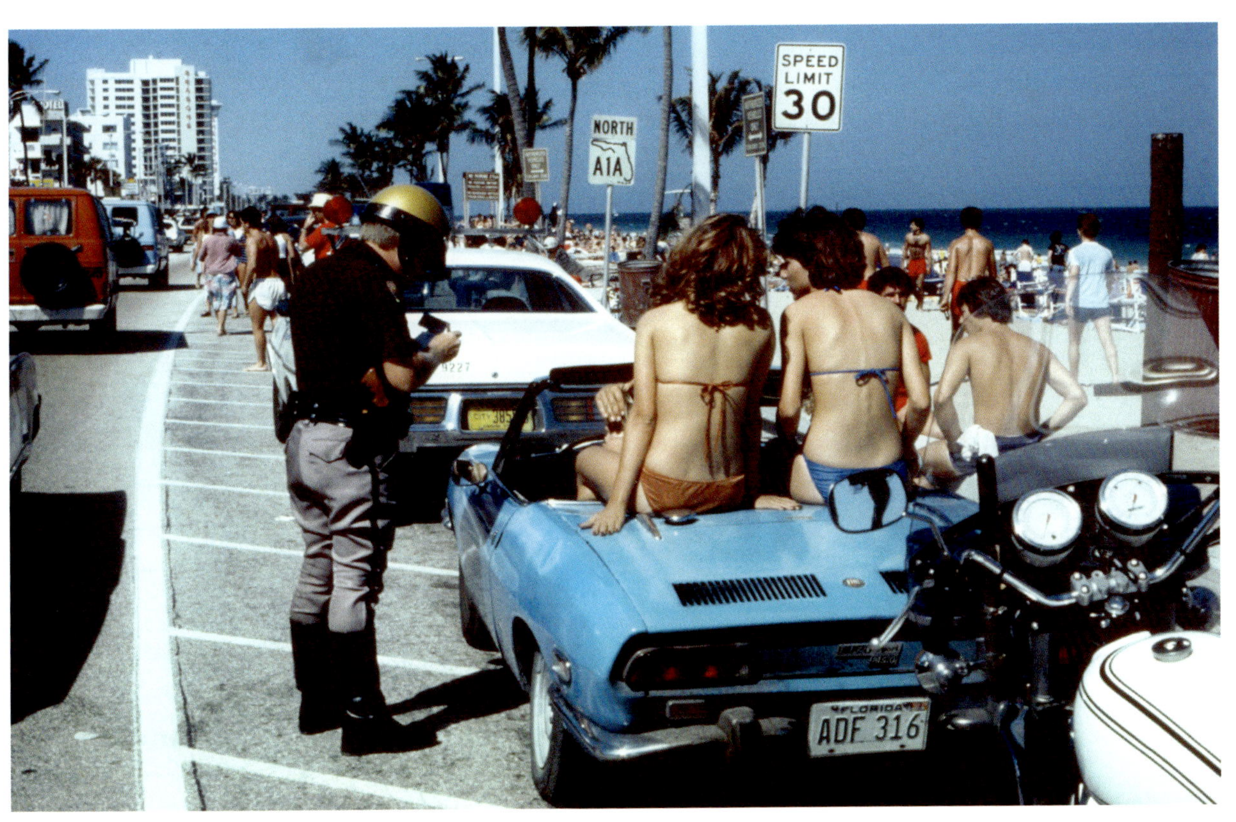

SPEED
LIMIT
30
NORTH
A1A
ADF 316
FLORIDA

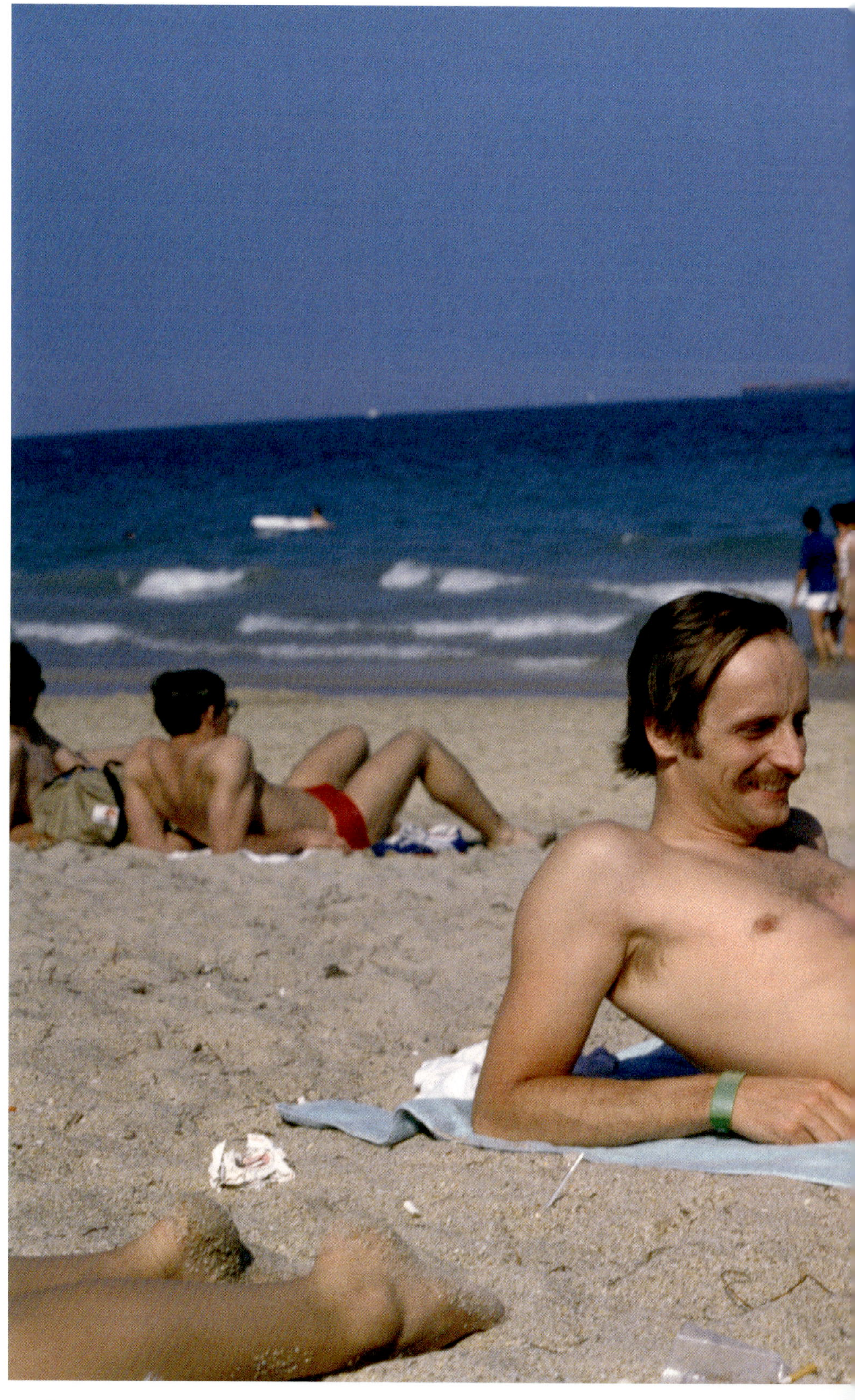

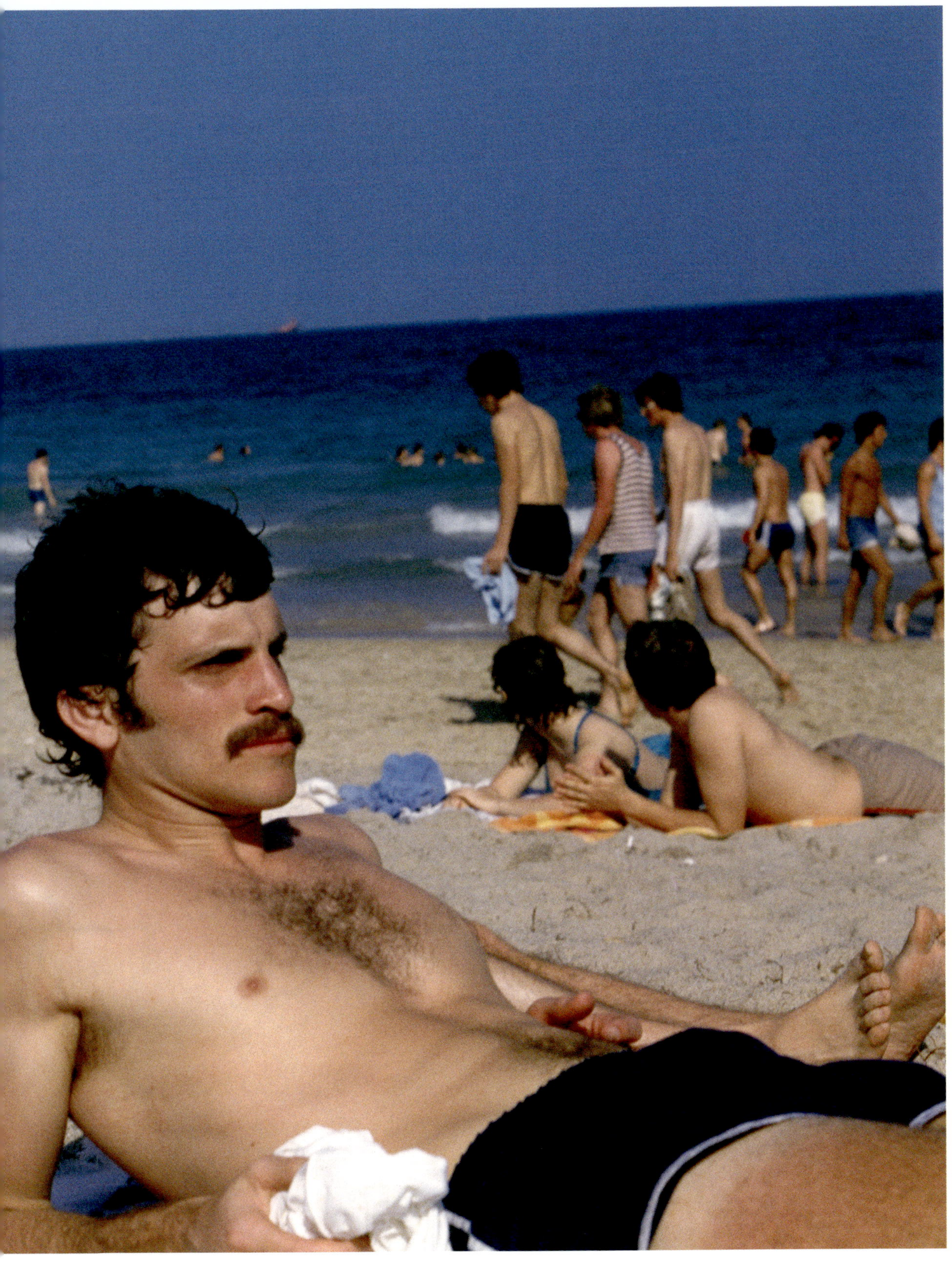

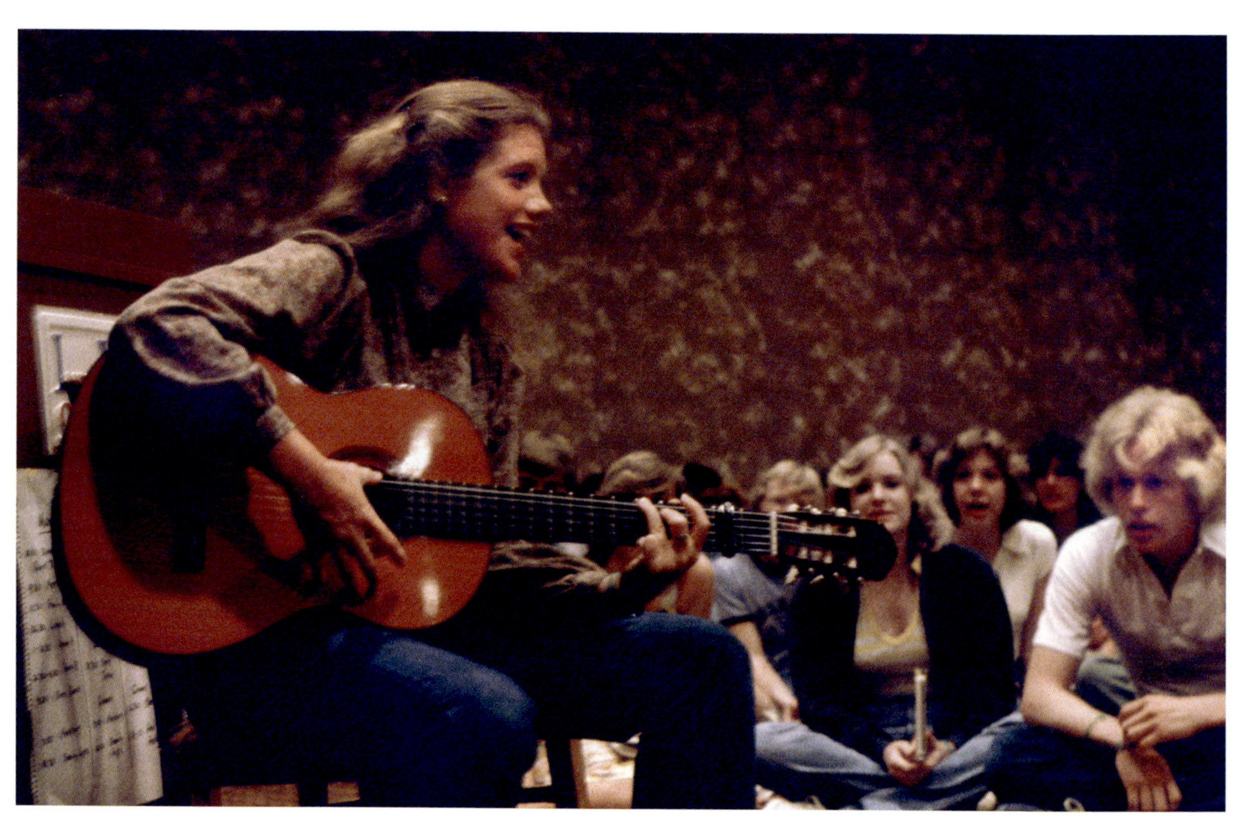

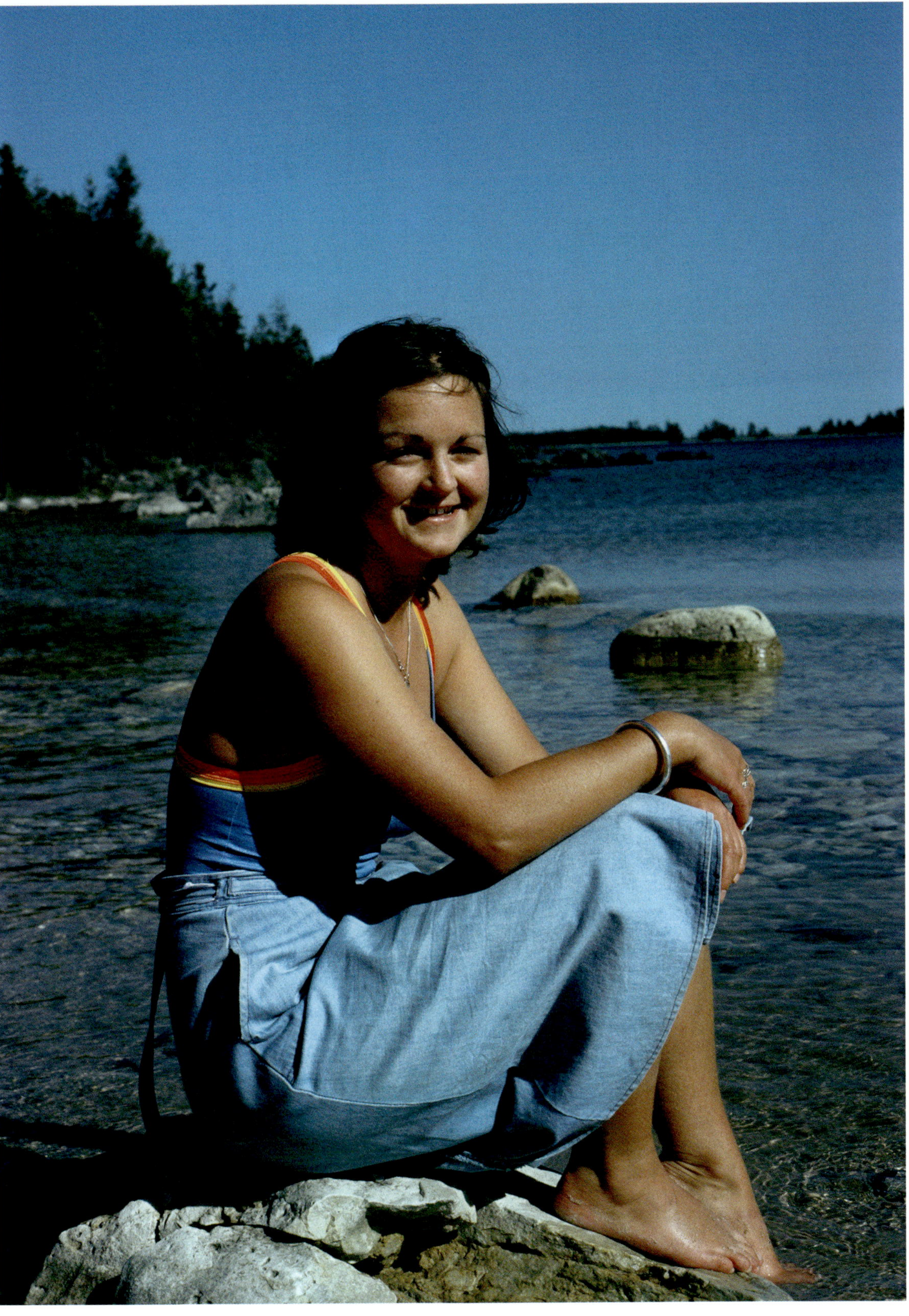

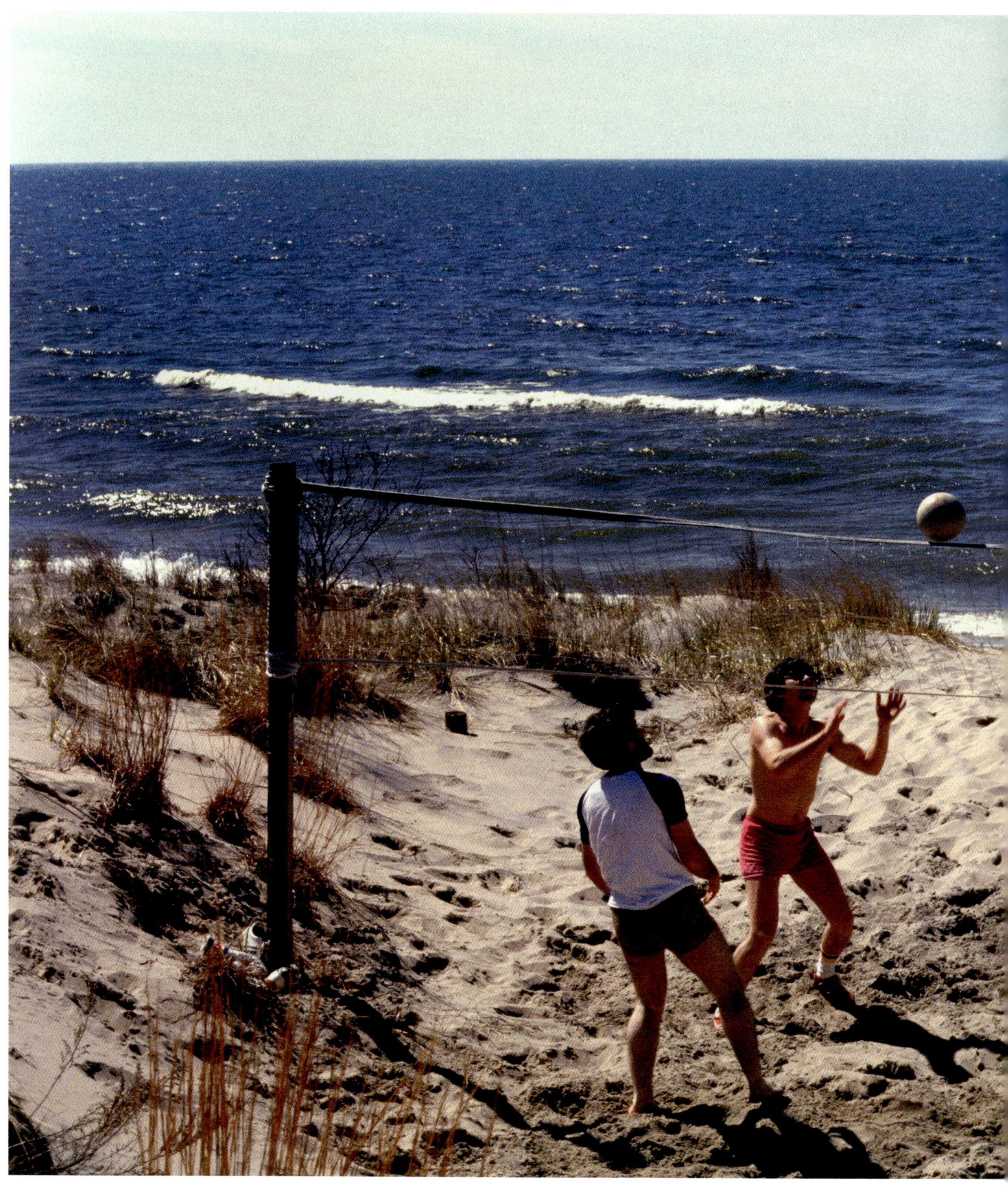

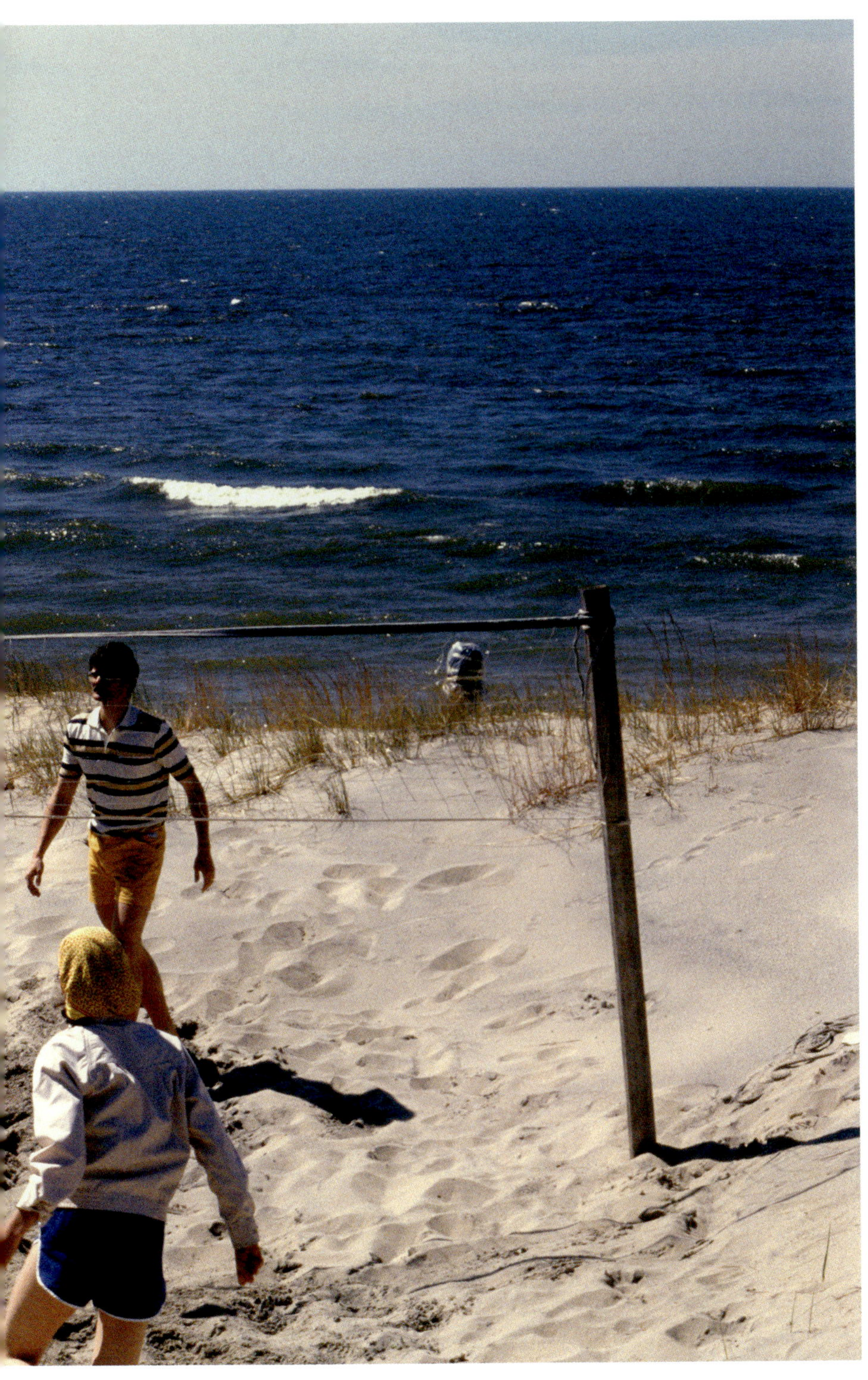

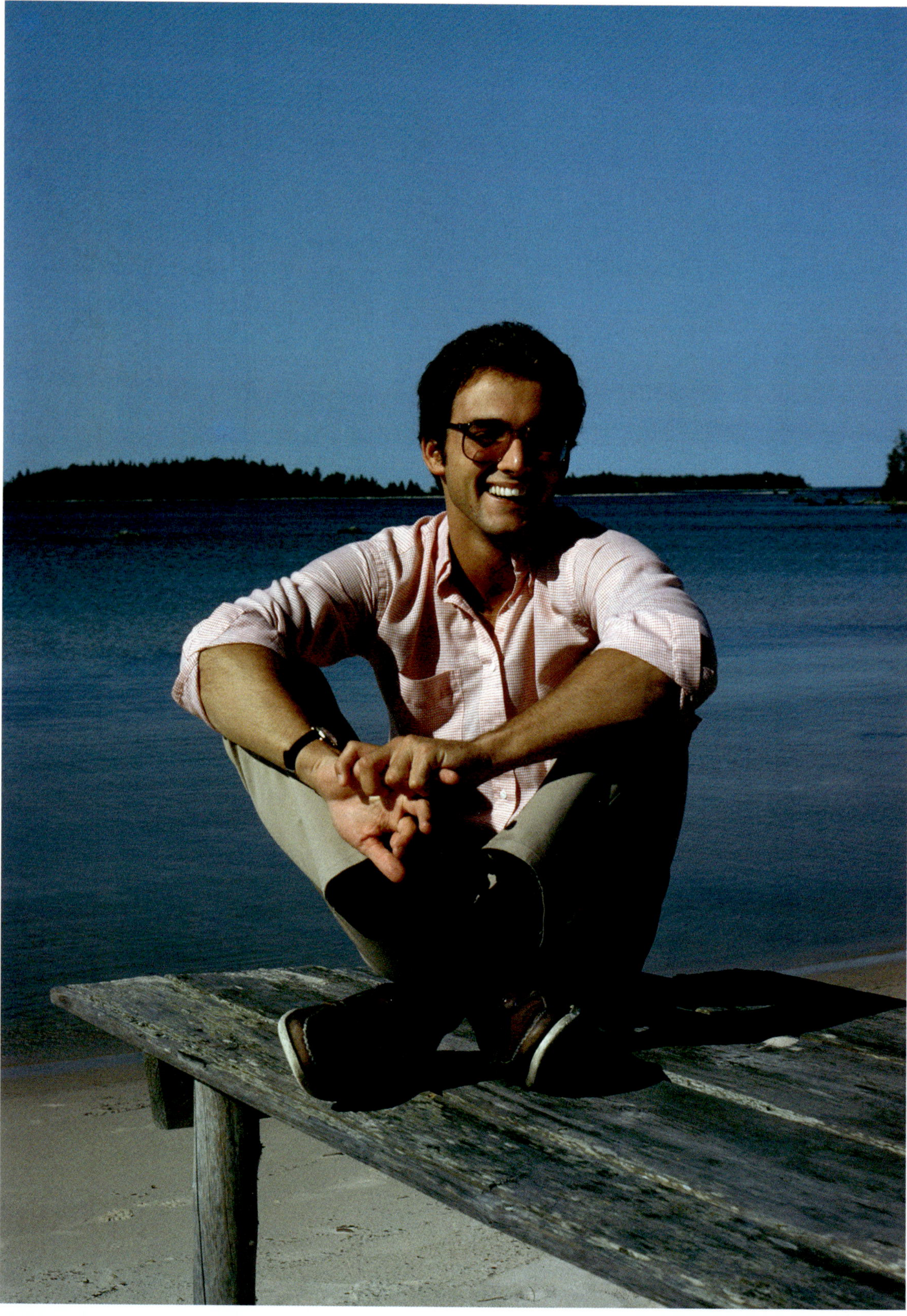

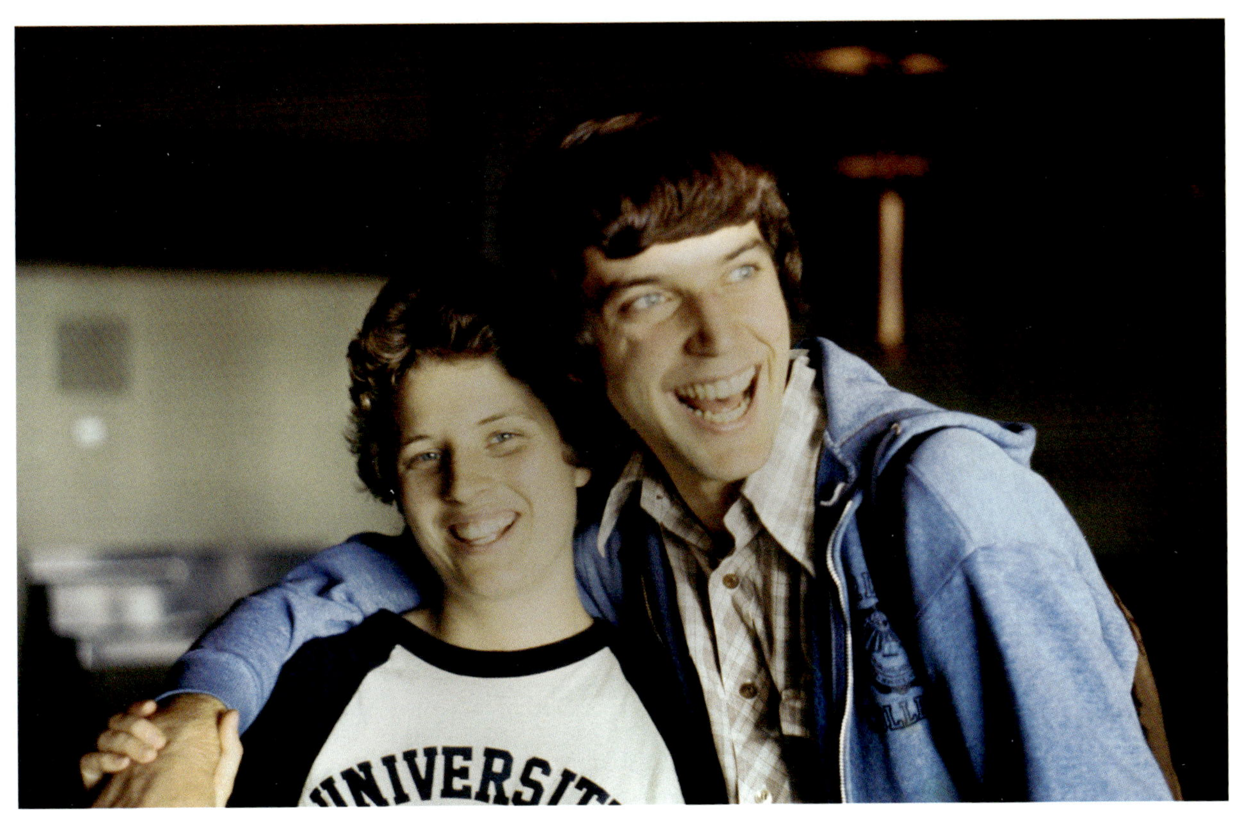

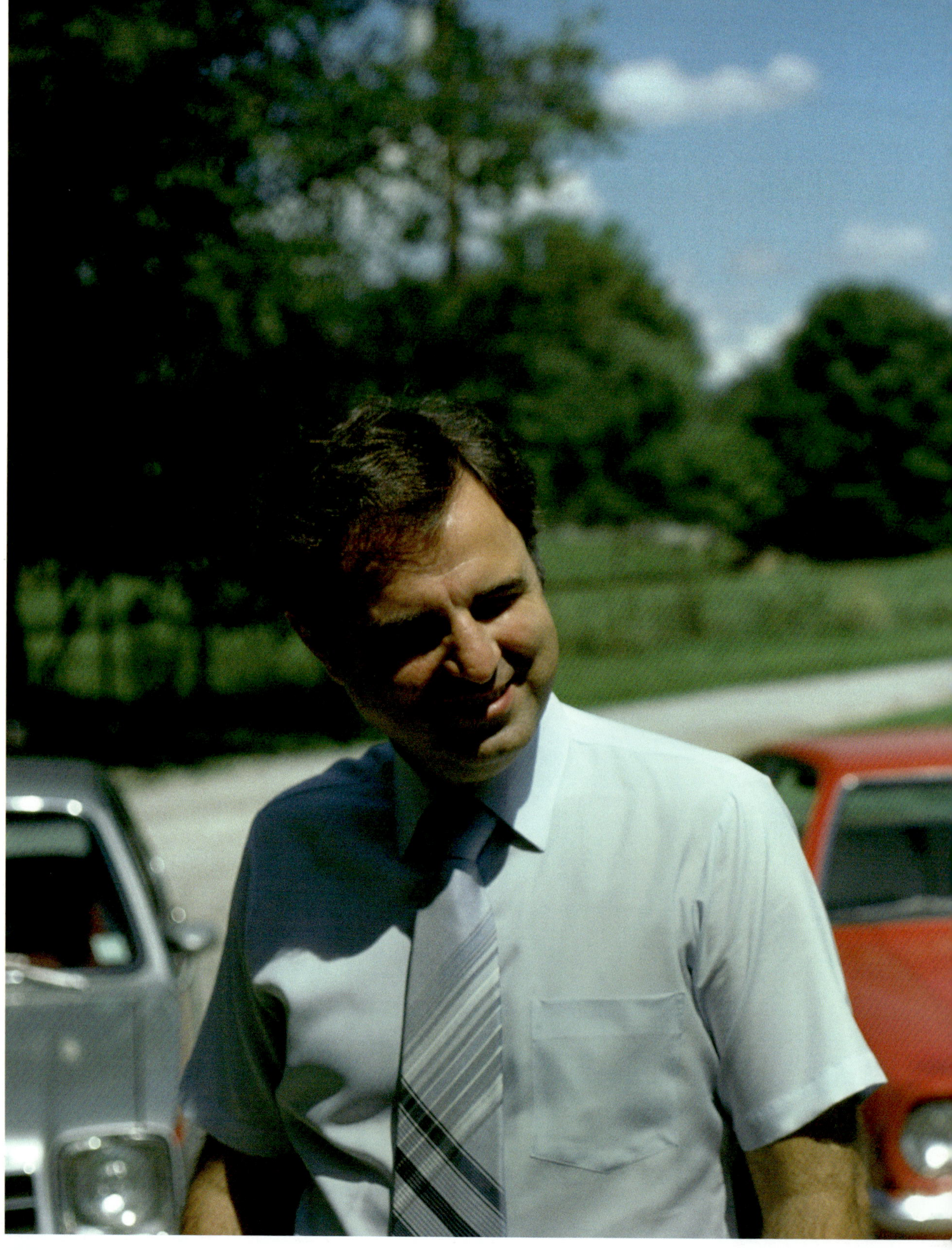

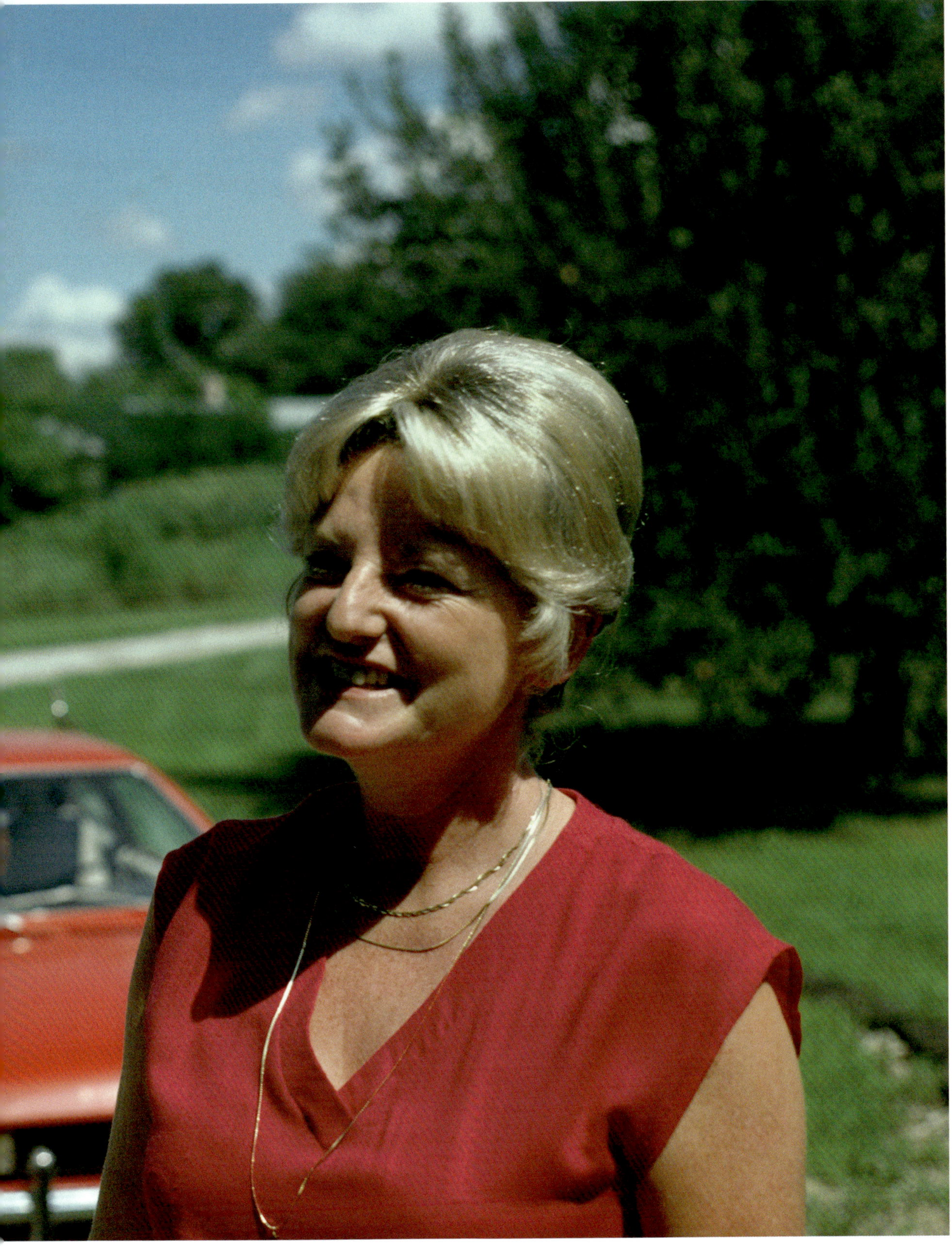

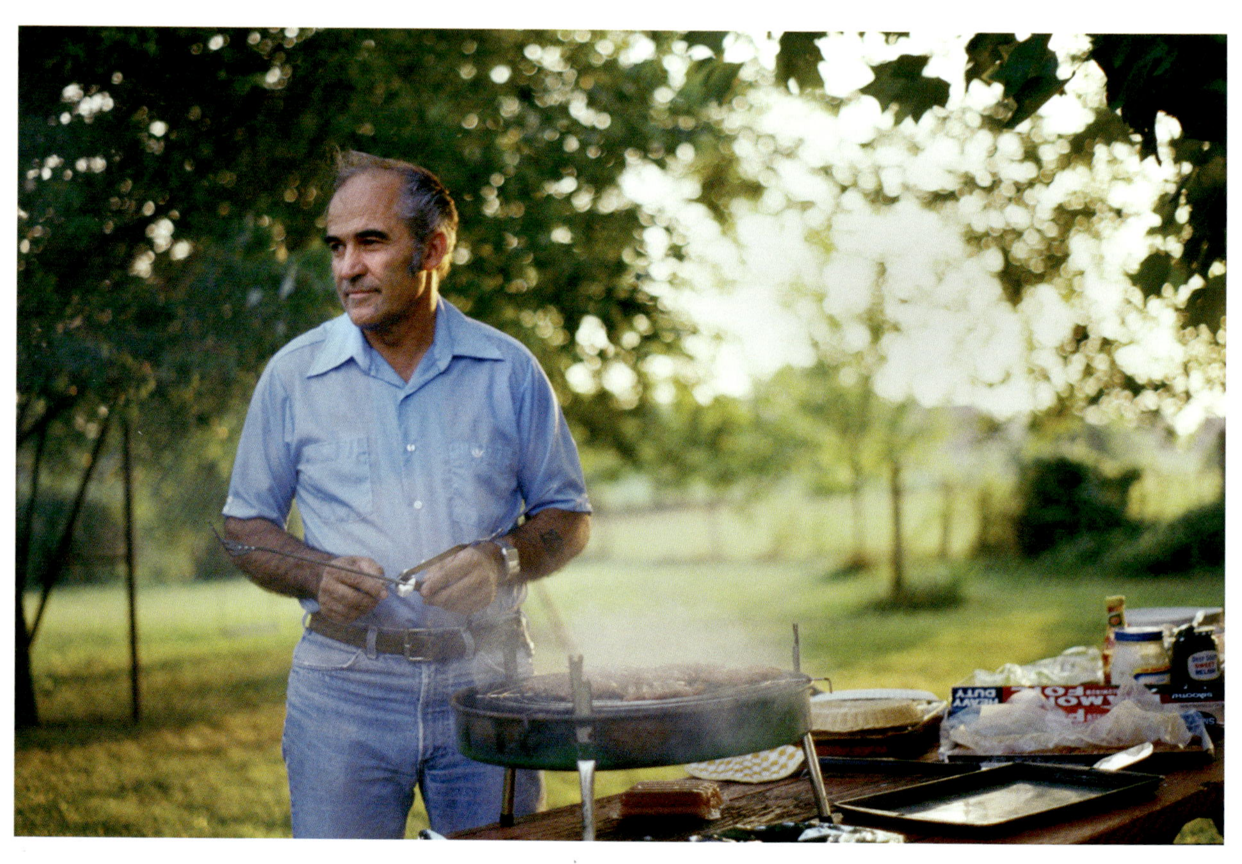

HEAVY
DUTY

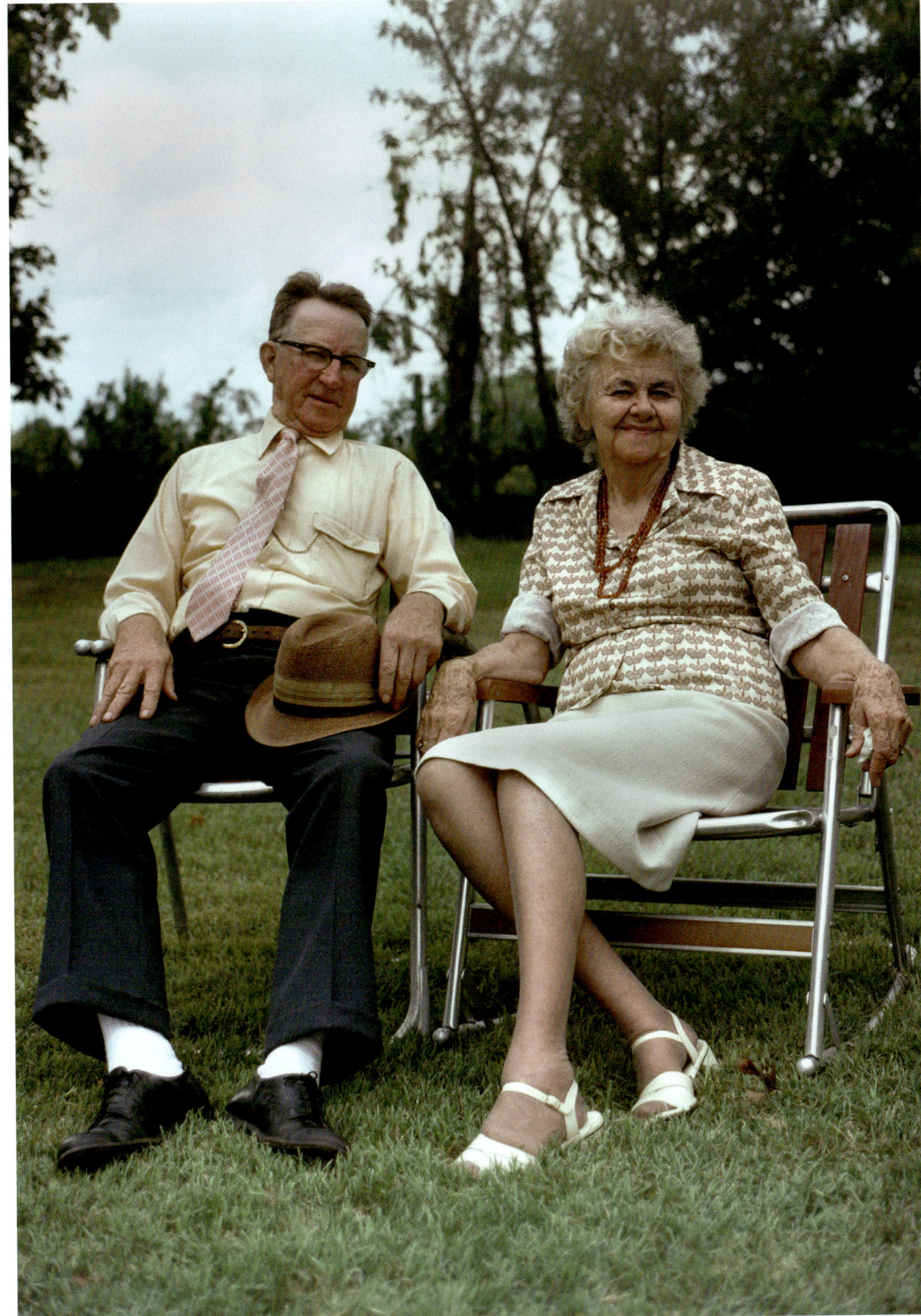

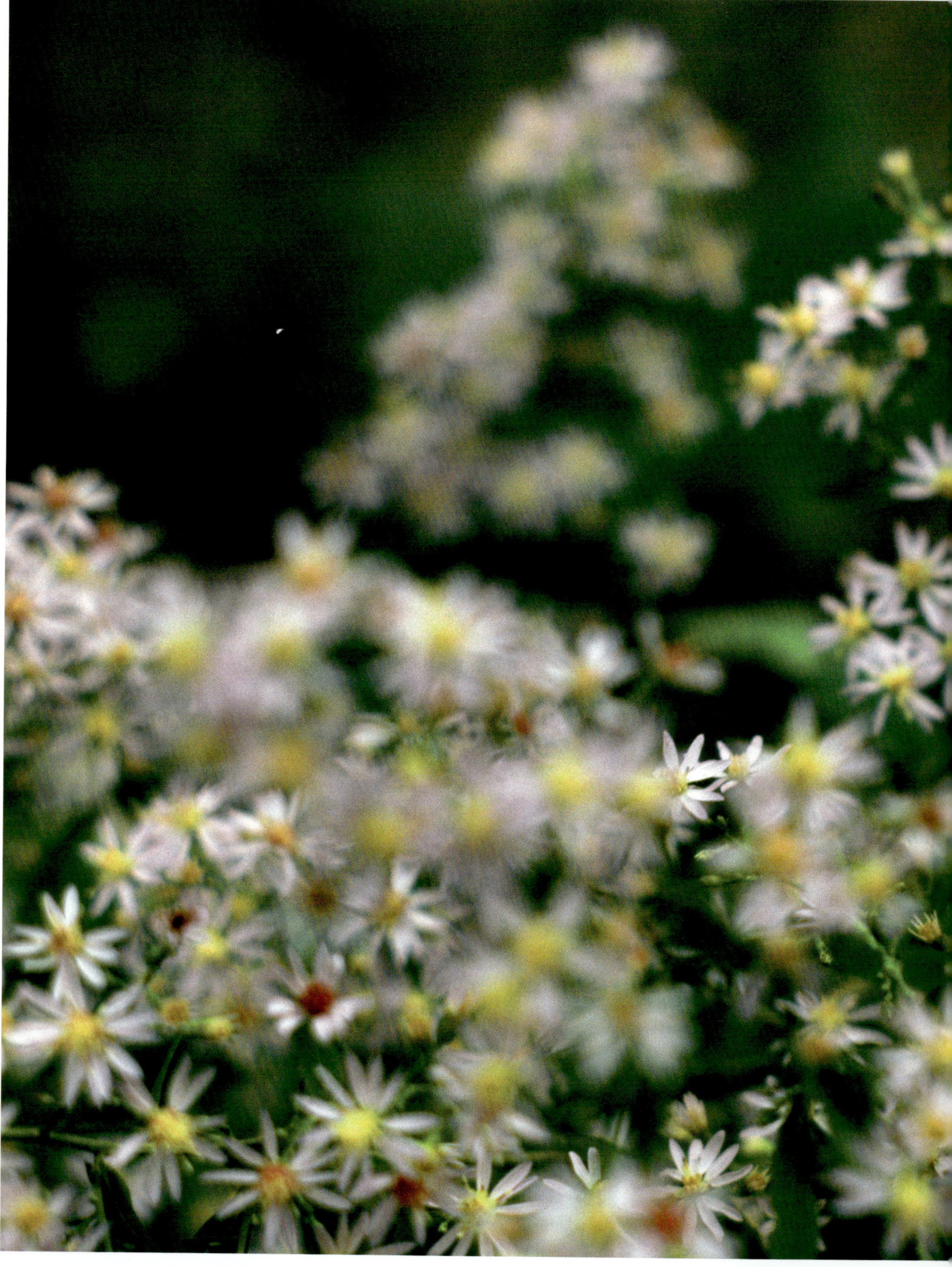

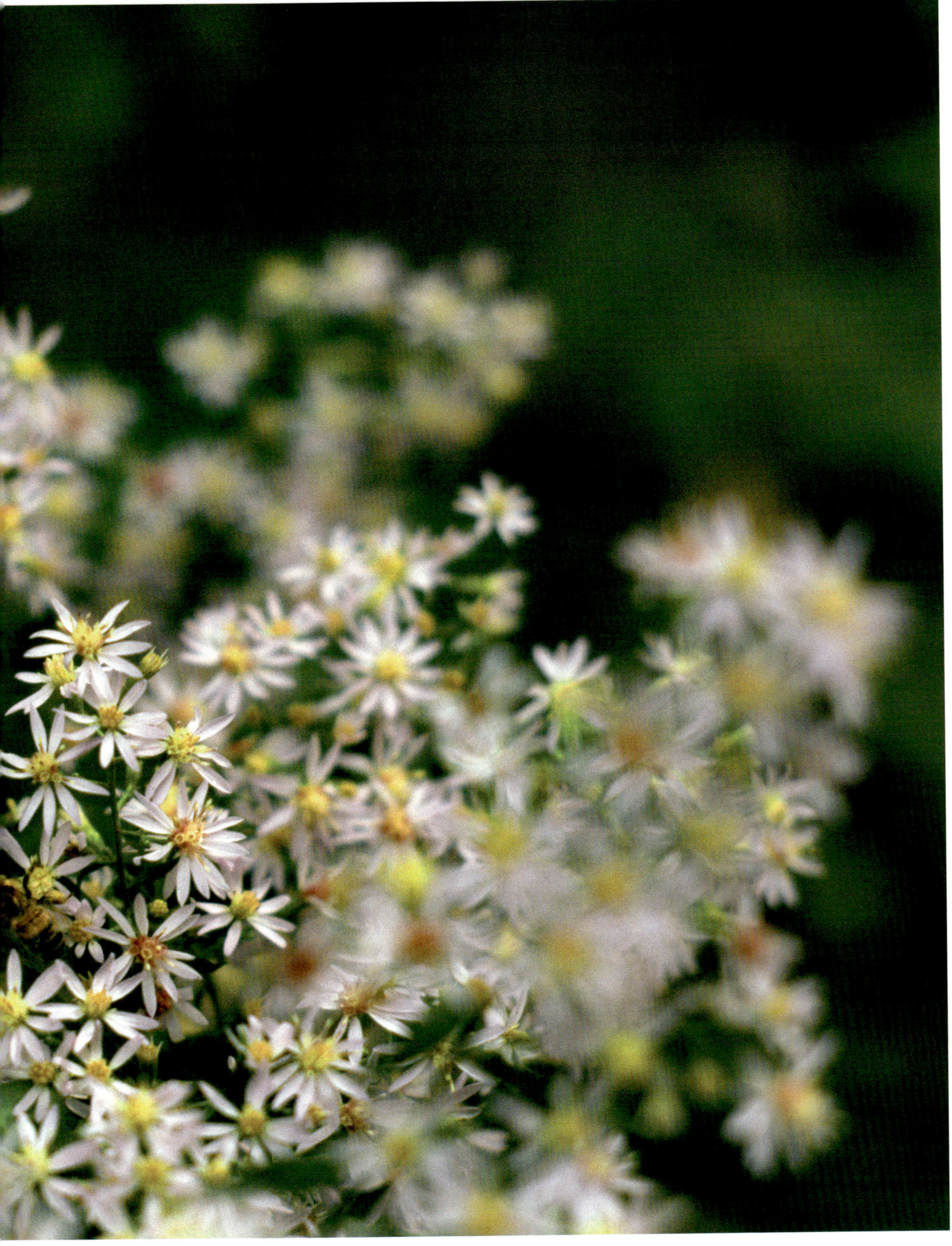

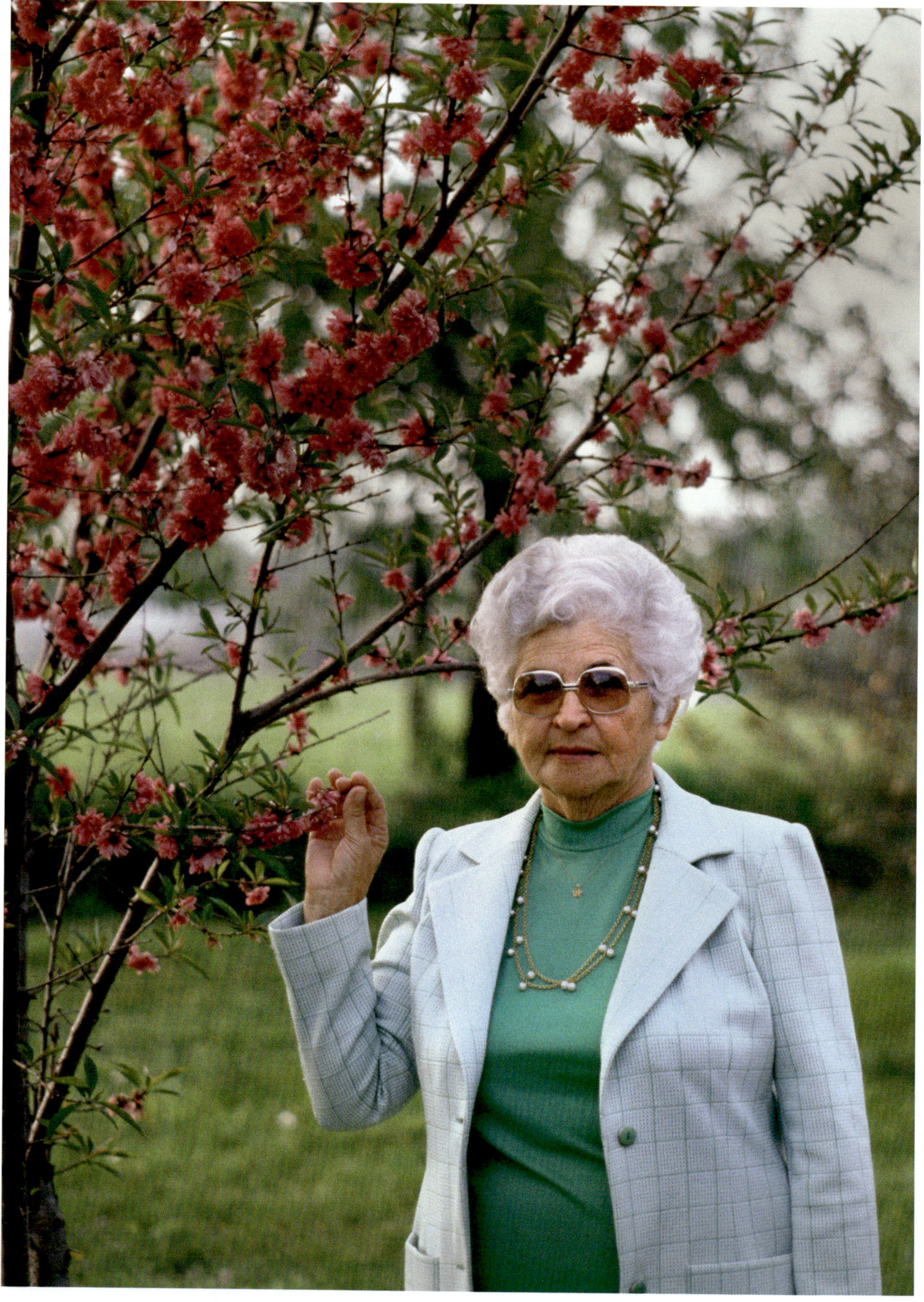

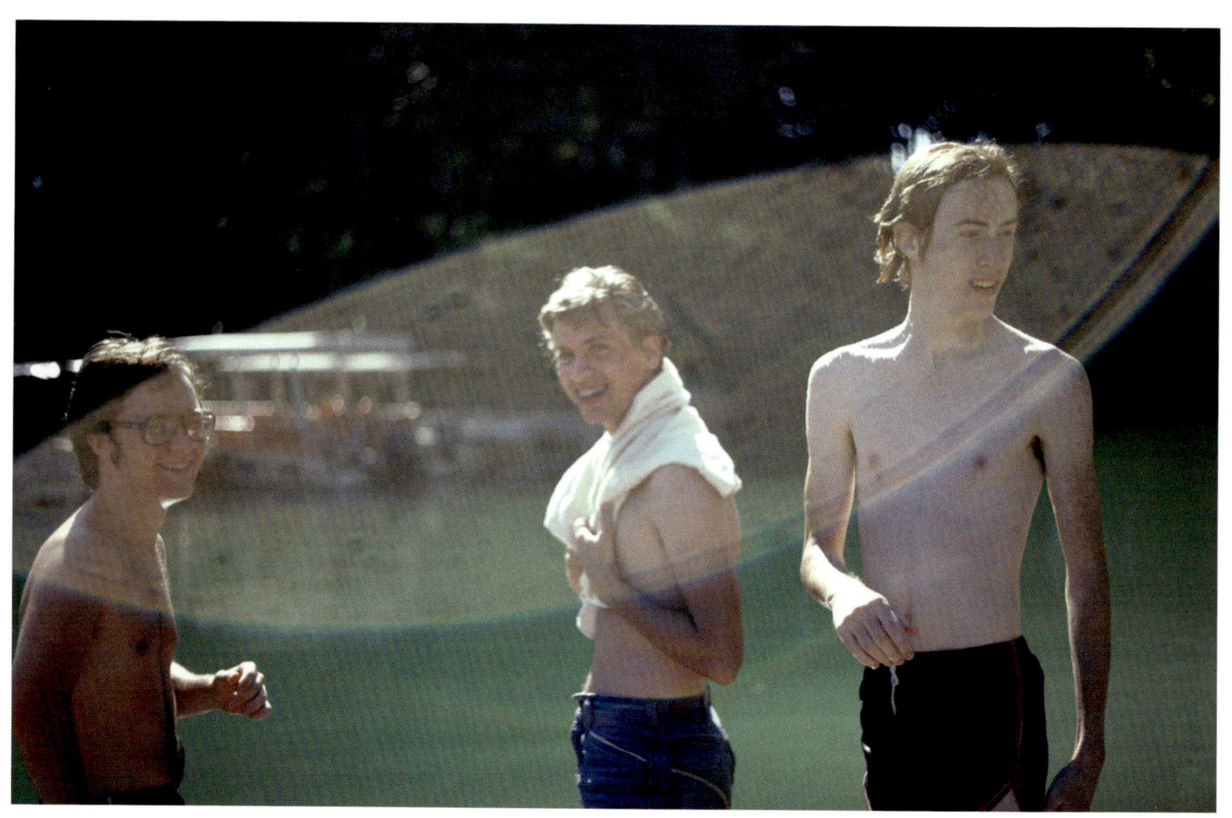

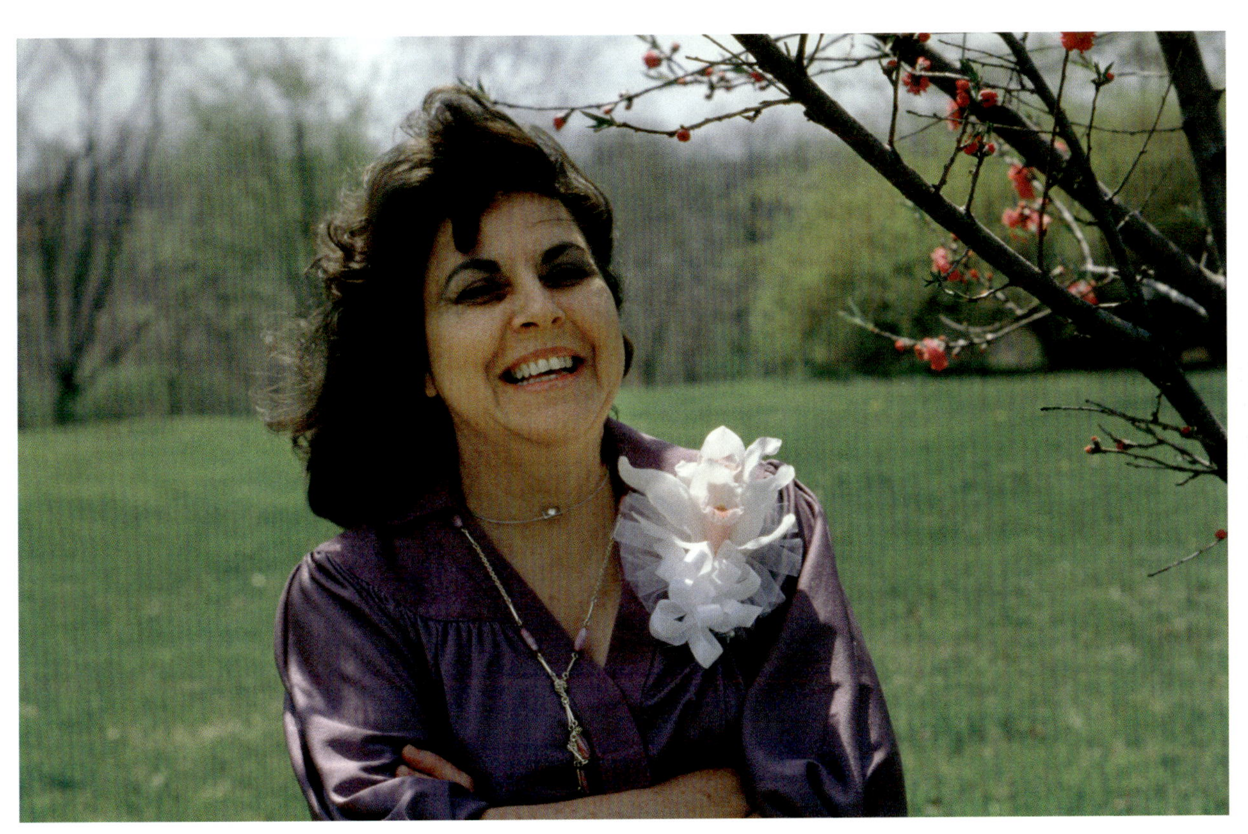

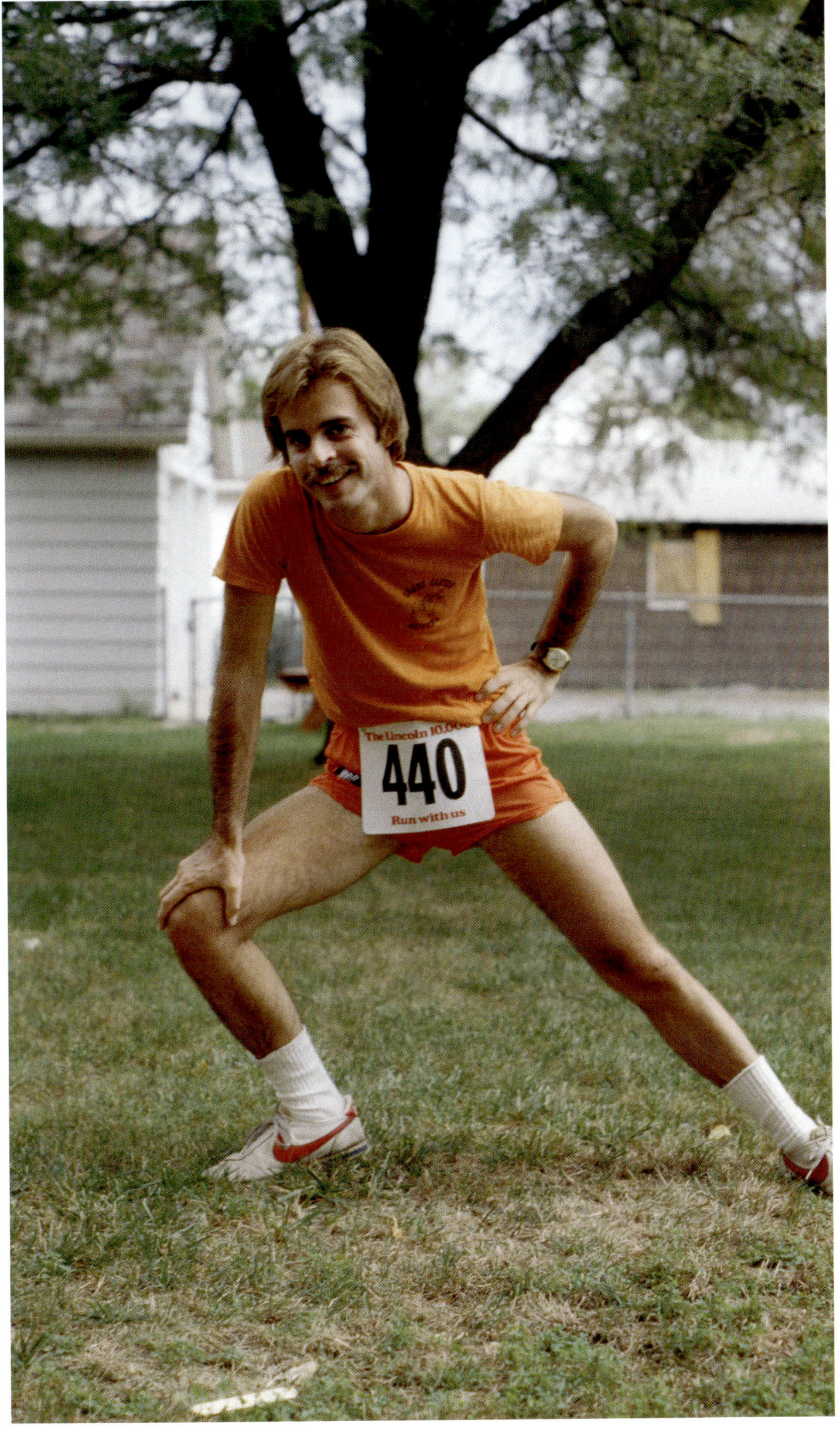
The Lincoln 10,000
440
Run with us

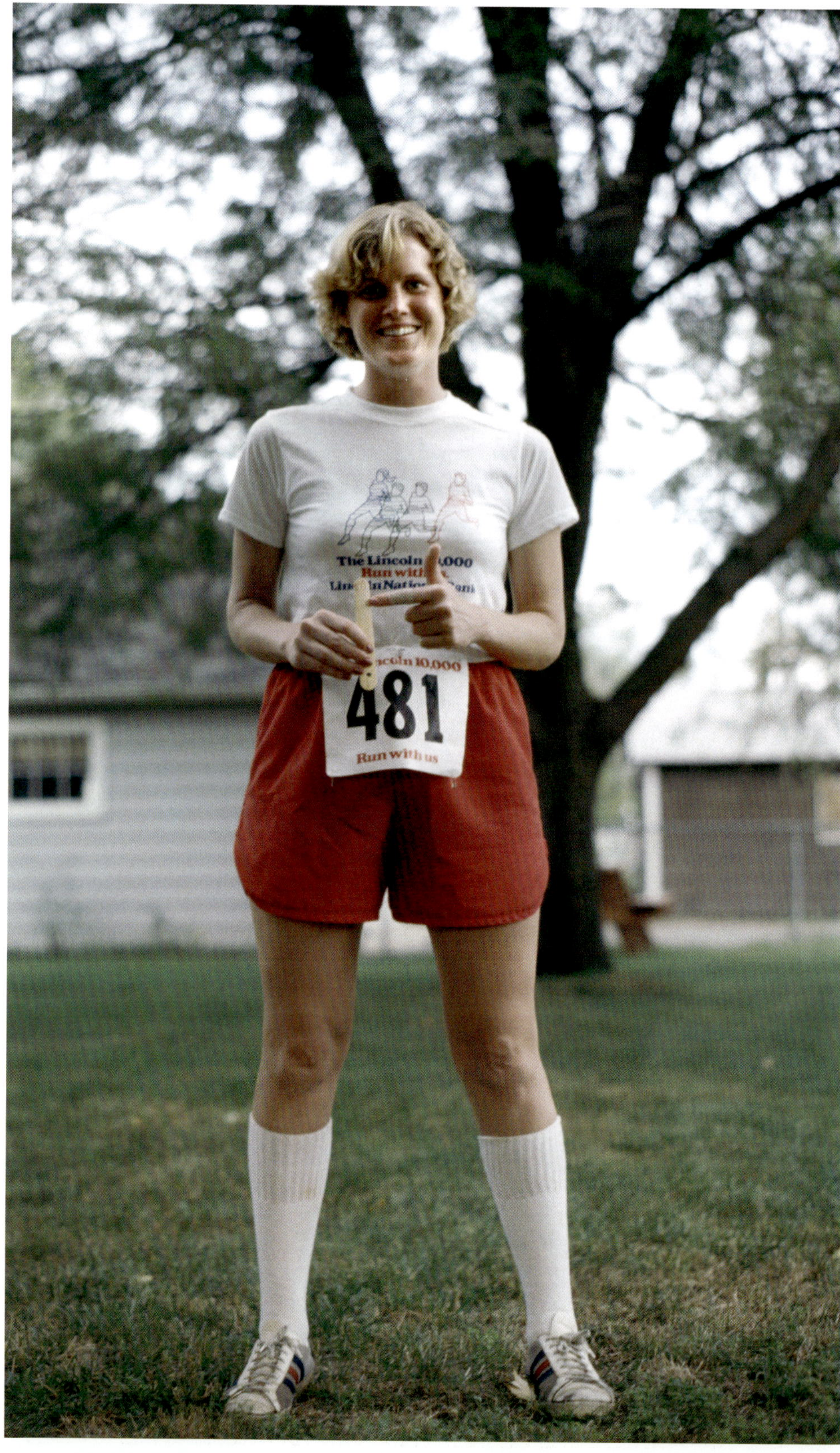
The Lincoln 10,000
Run with us
Lincoln National Bank
Lincoln 10,000
481
Run with us

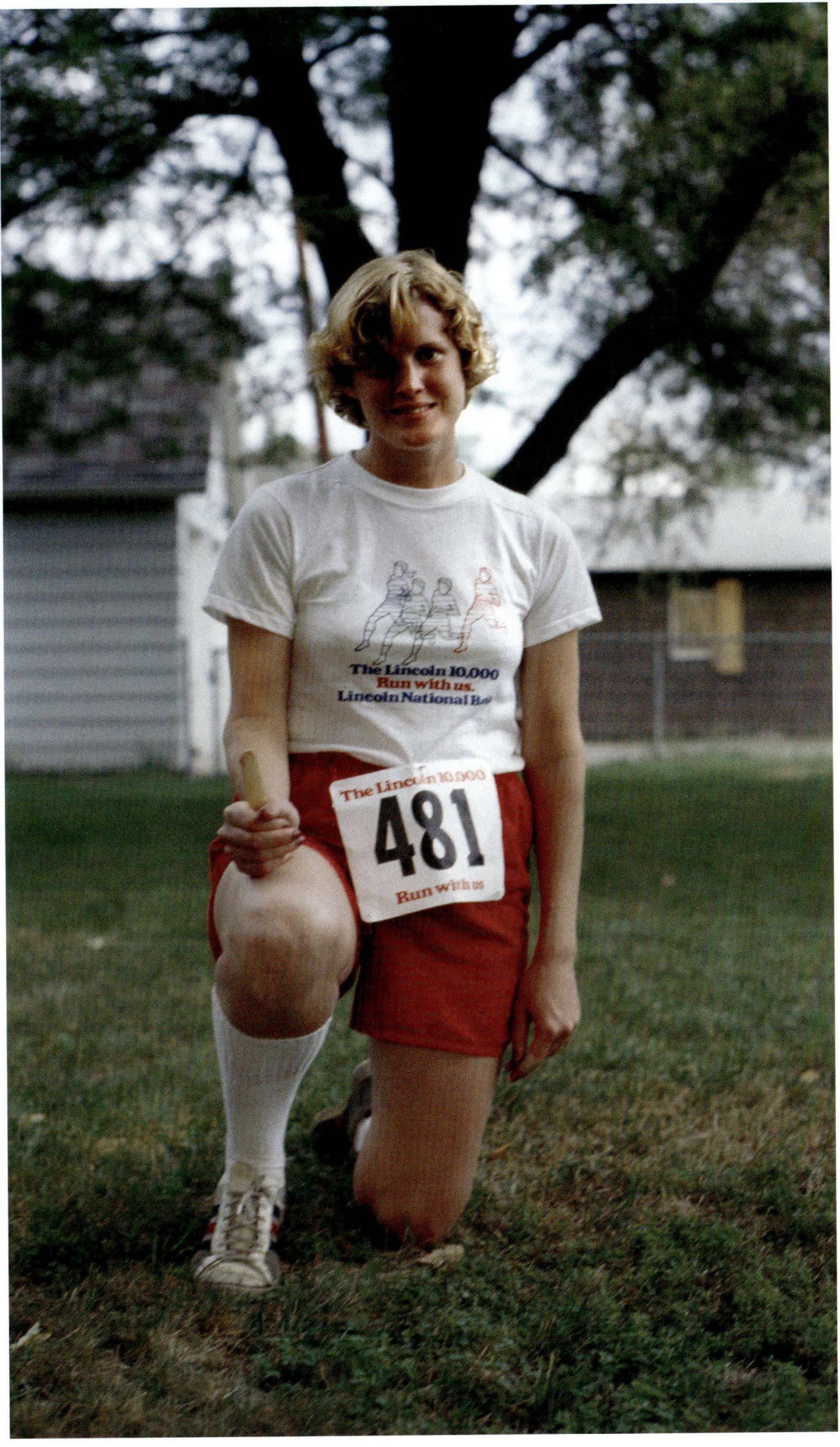
The Lincoln 10,000
Run with us.
Lincoln National B...
The Lincoln 10,000
481
Run with us

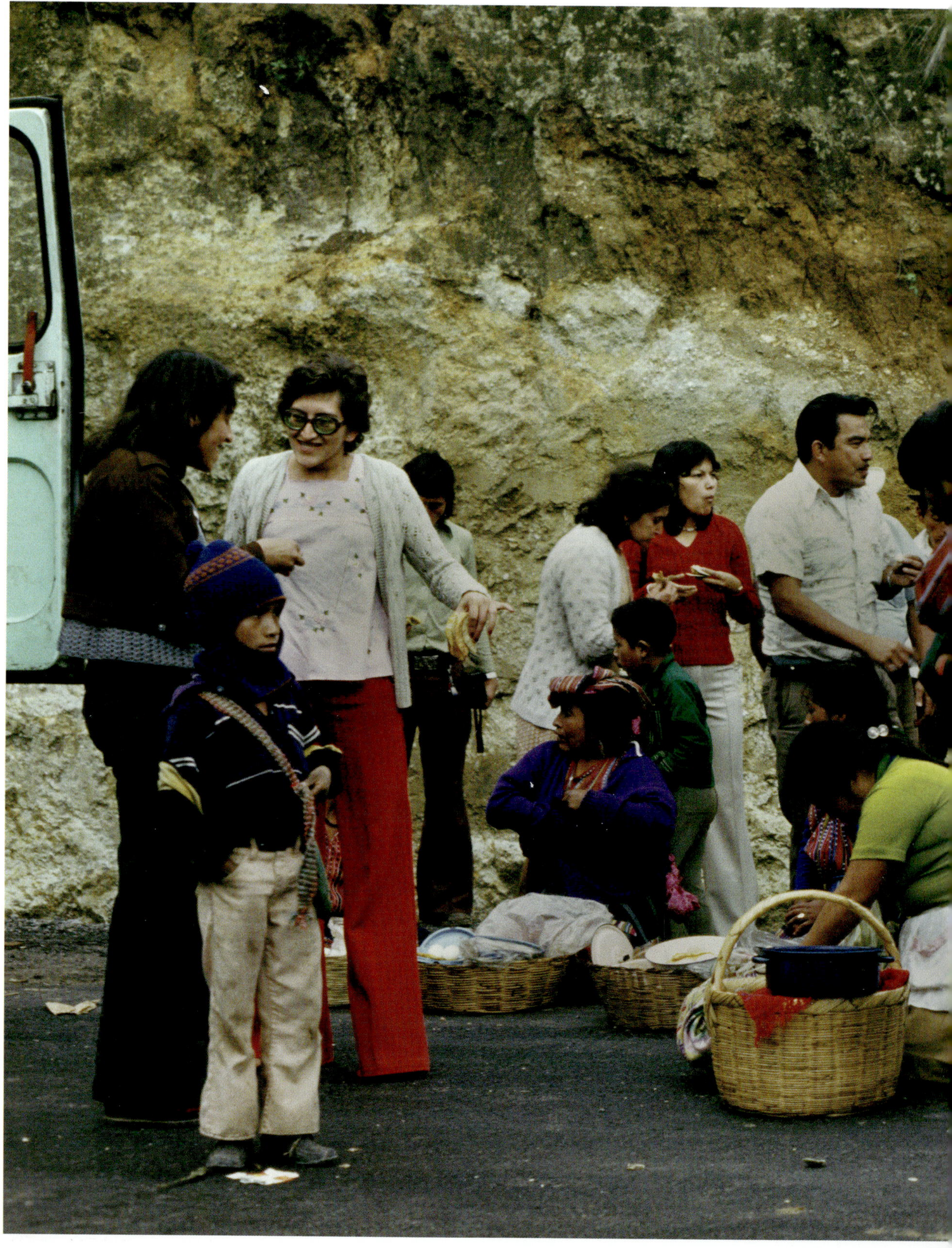

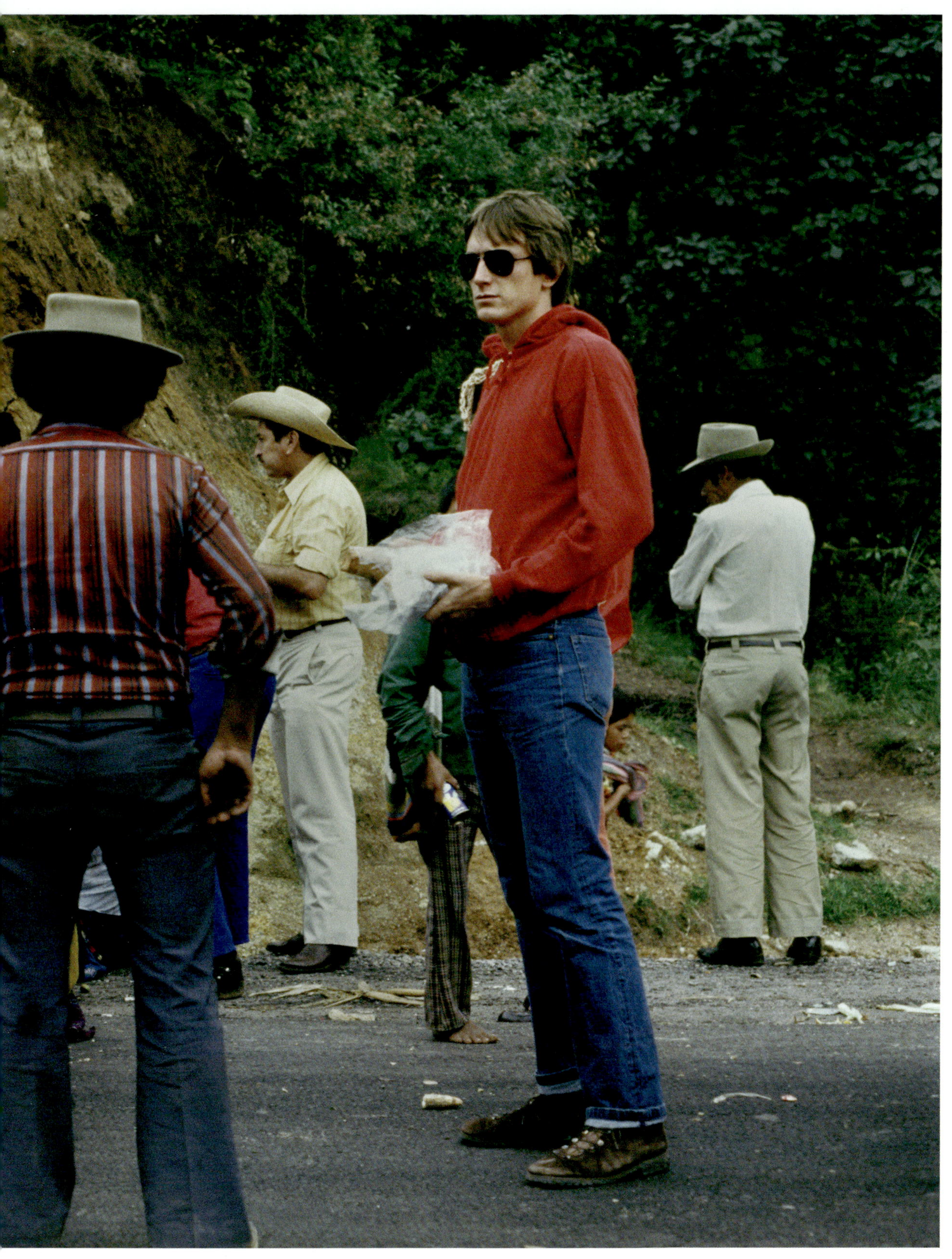

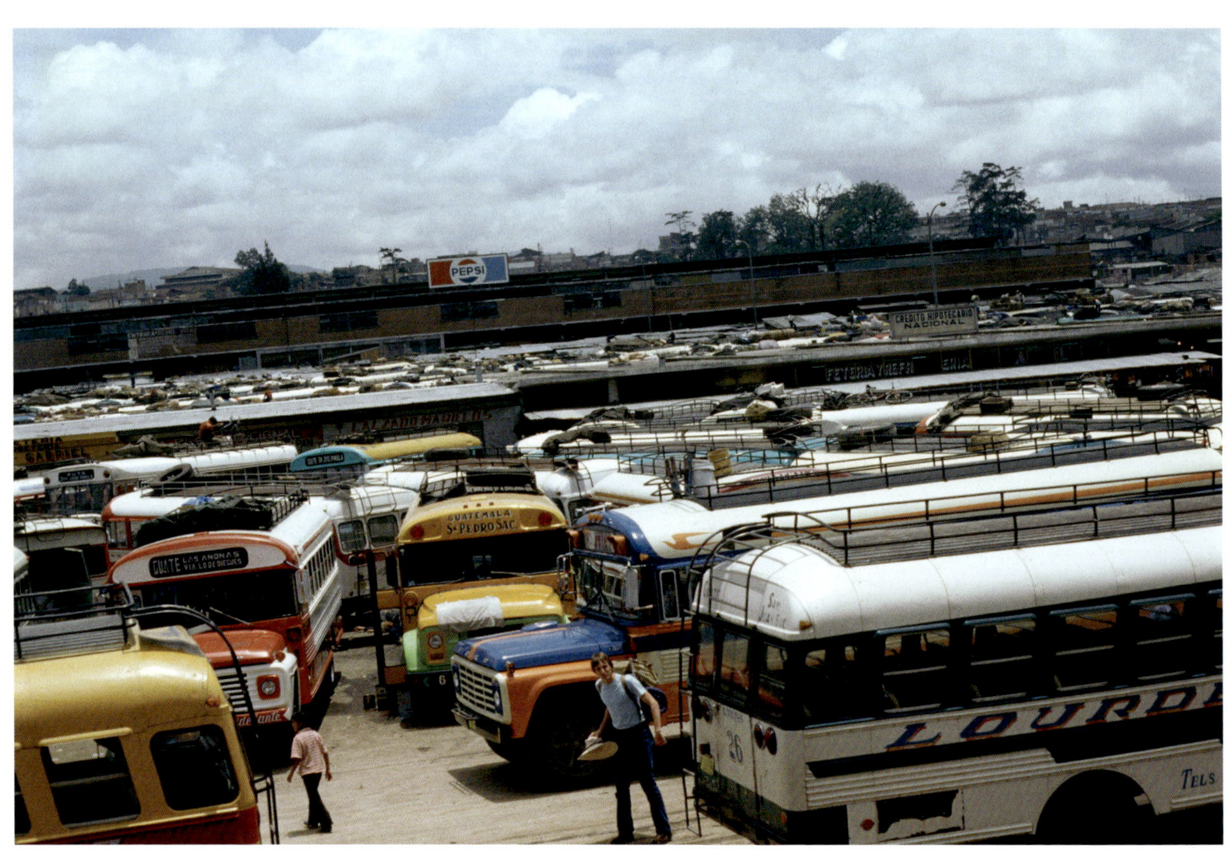

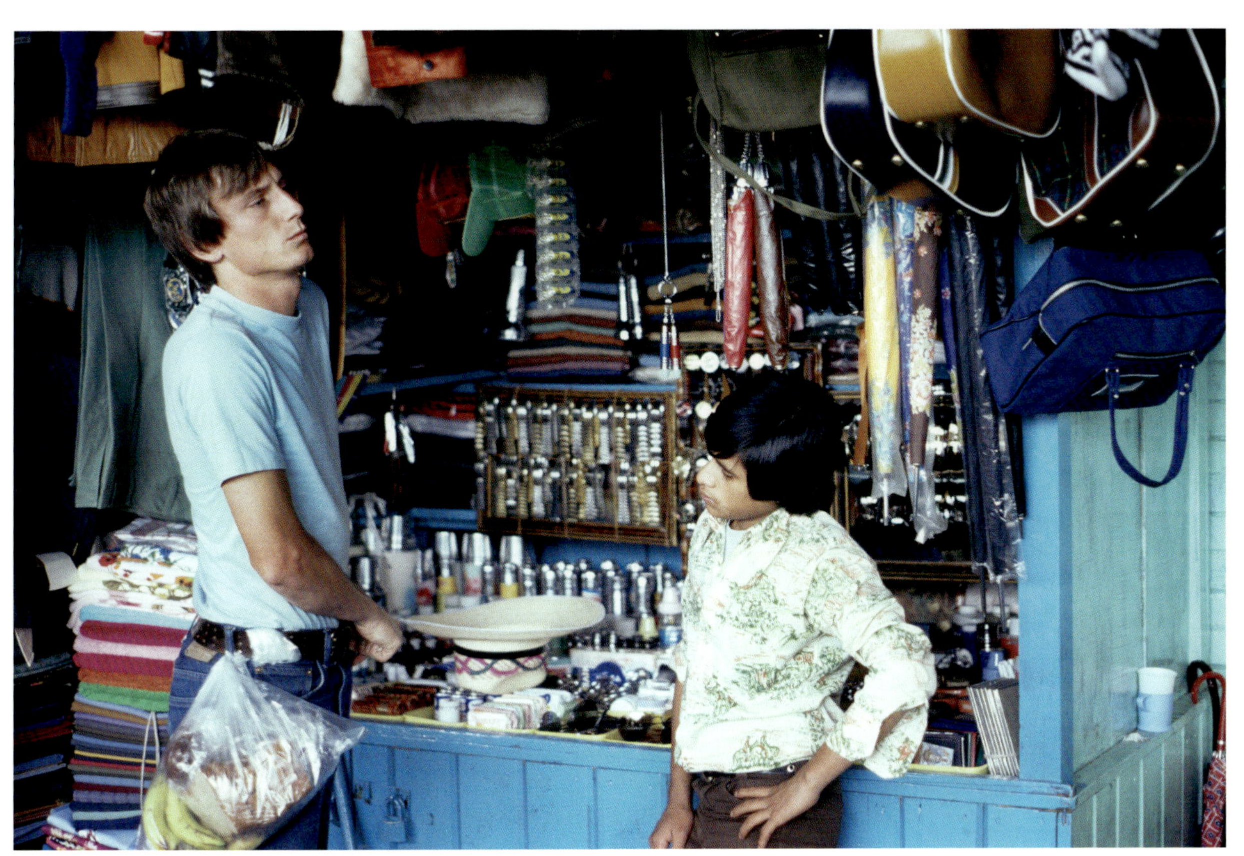

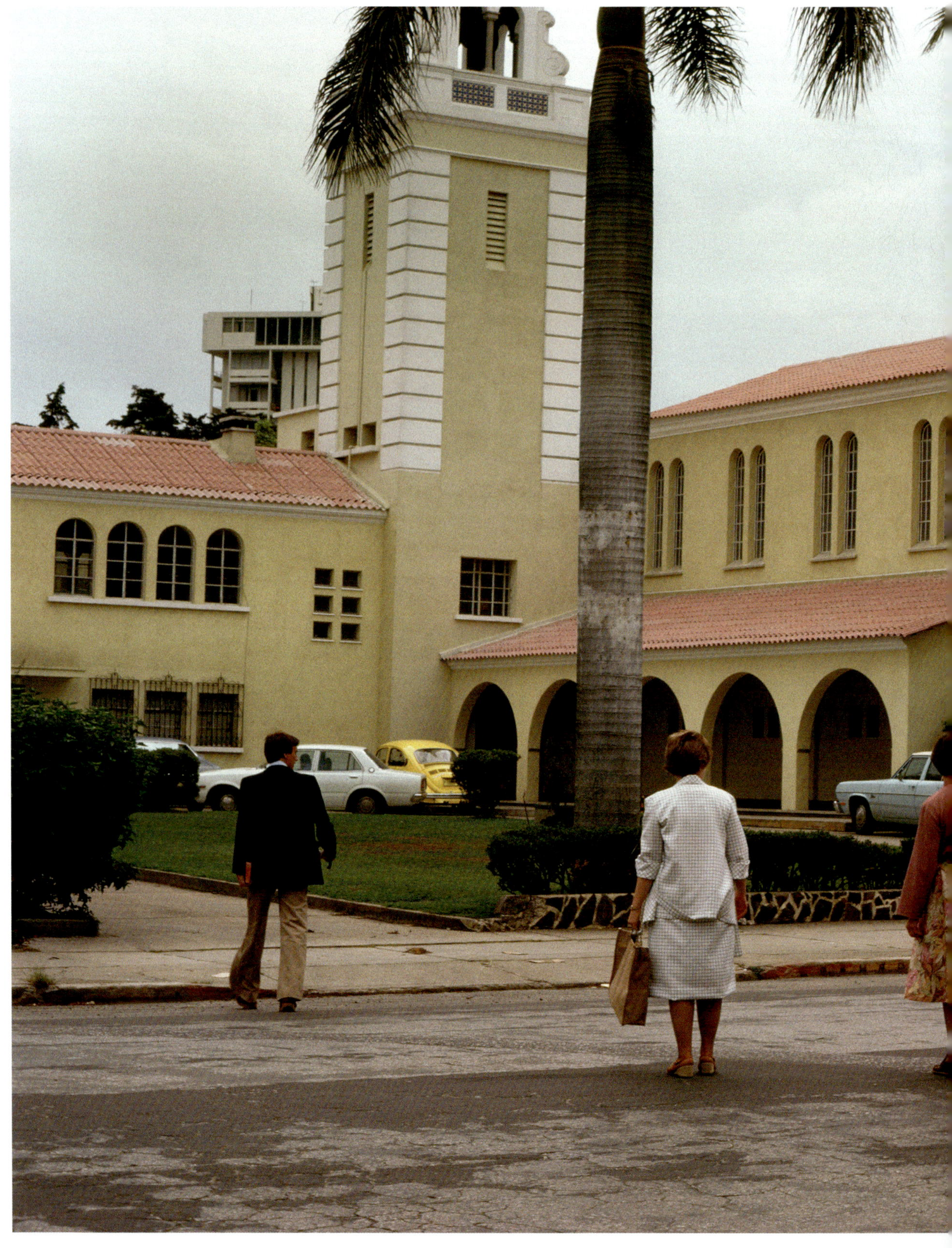

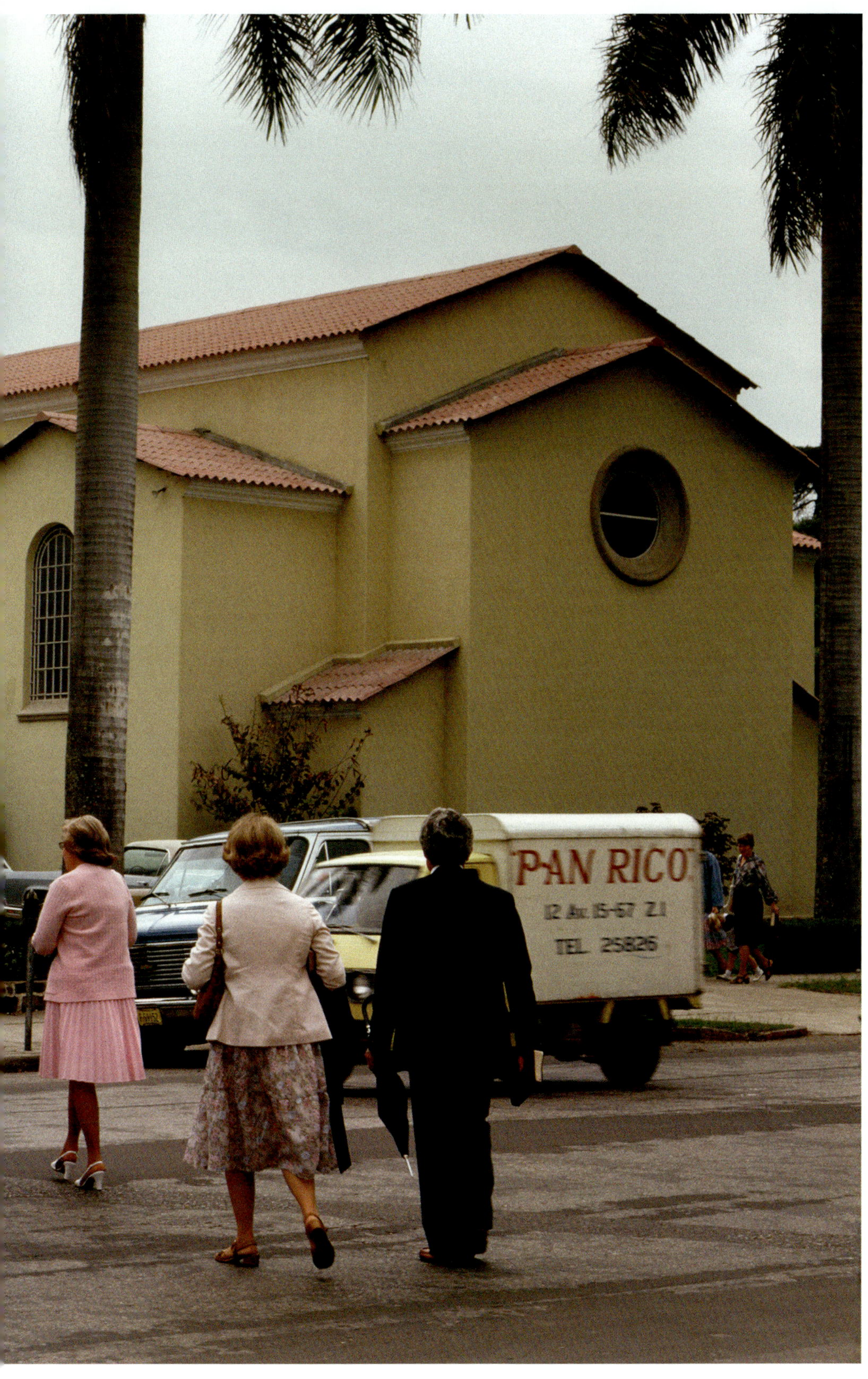
PAN RICO
12 Av. 15-67 Z.1
TEL. 25826

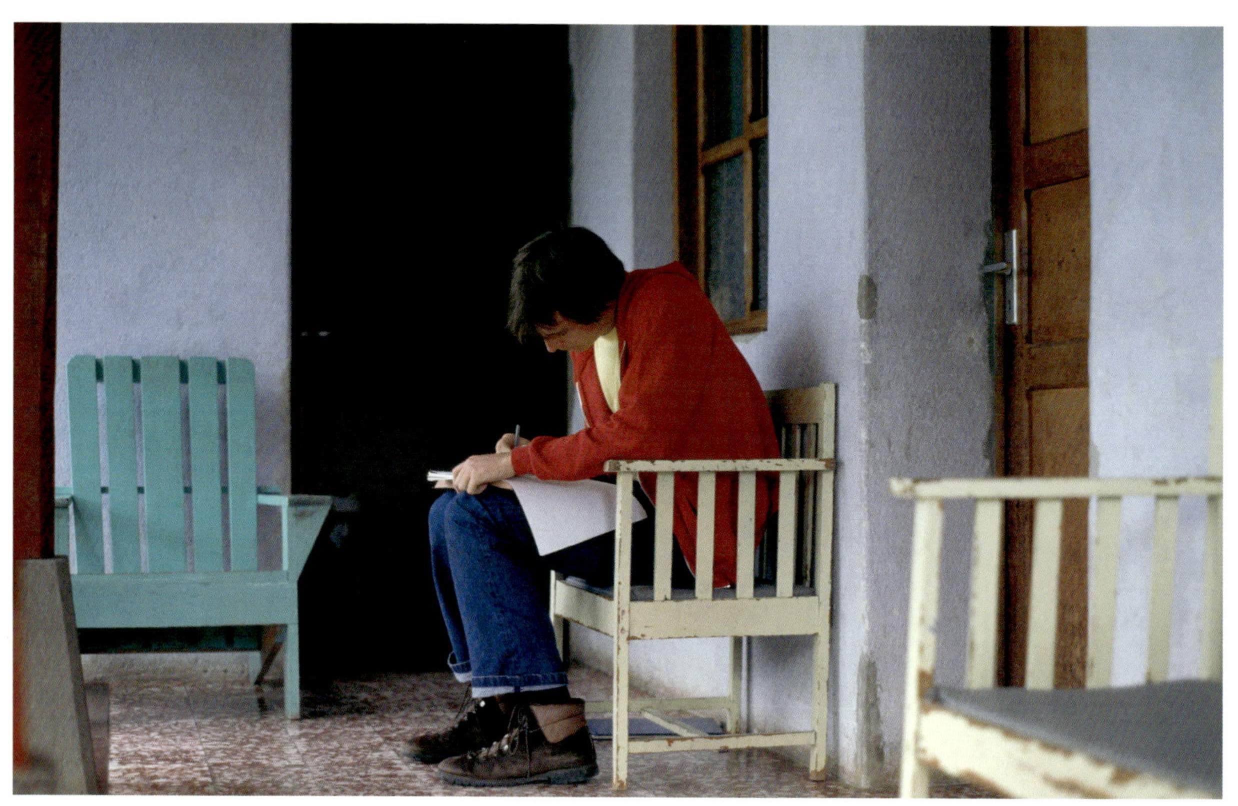

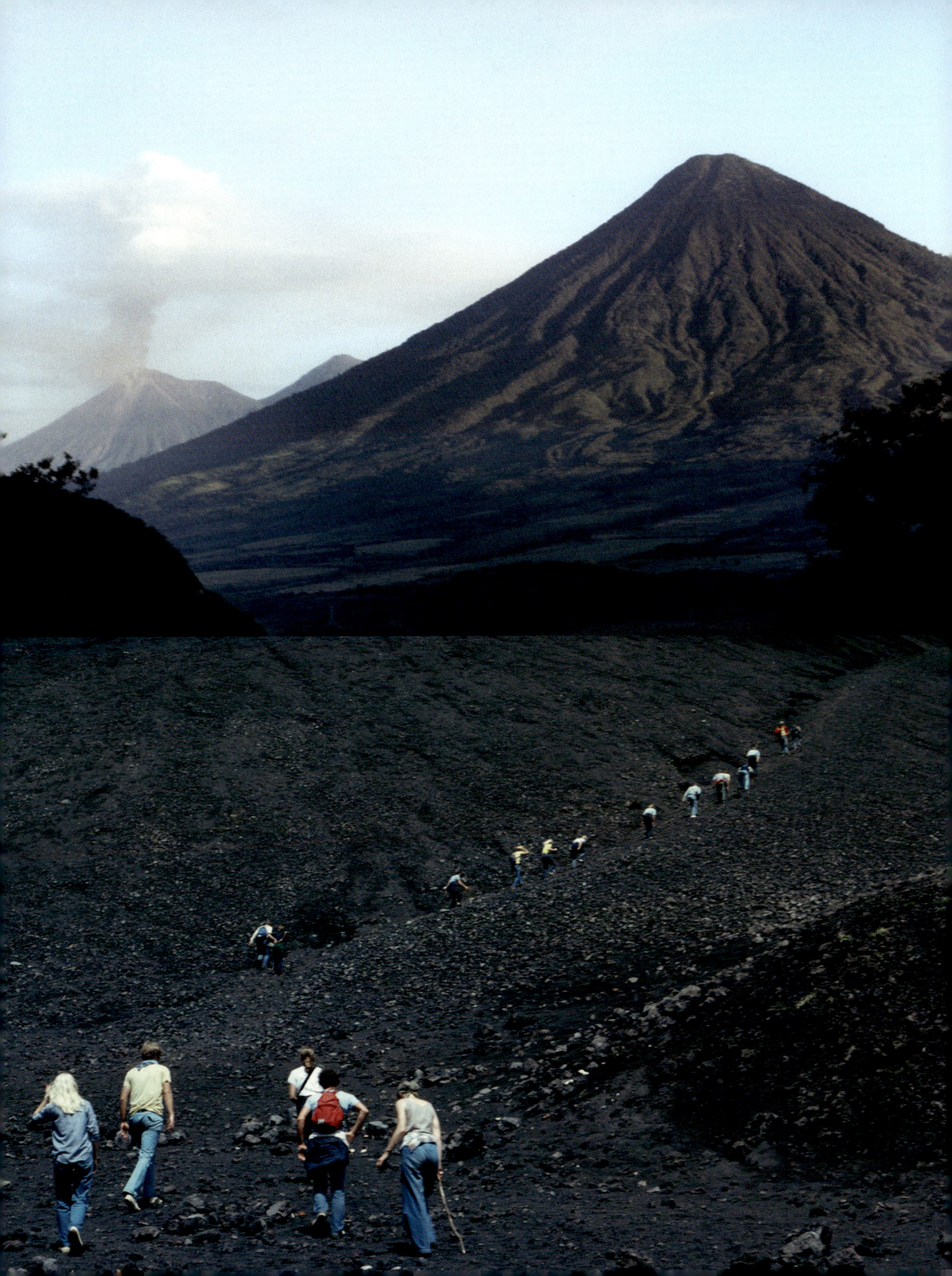

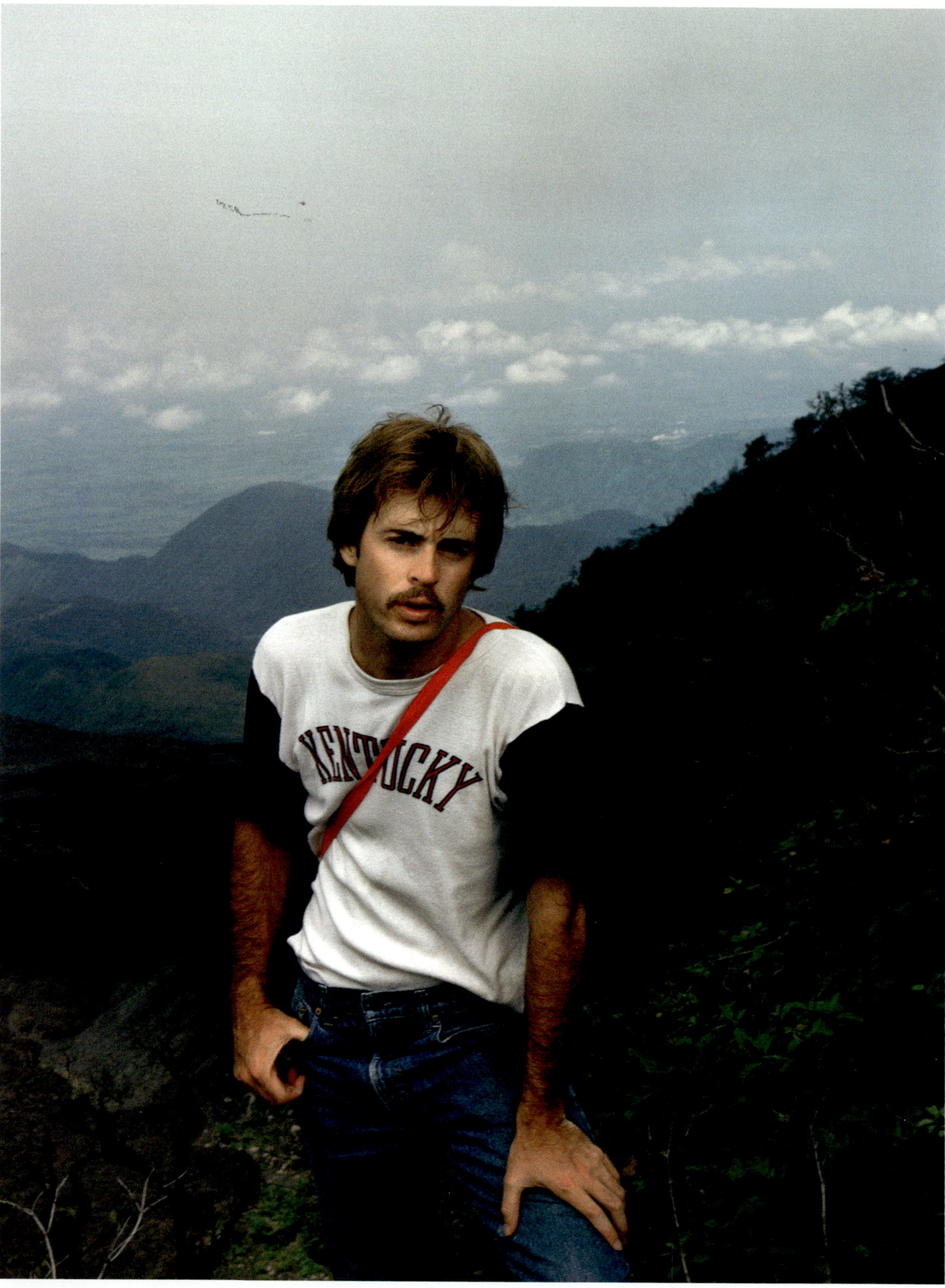
KENTUCKY

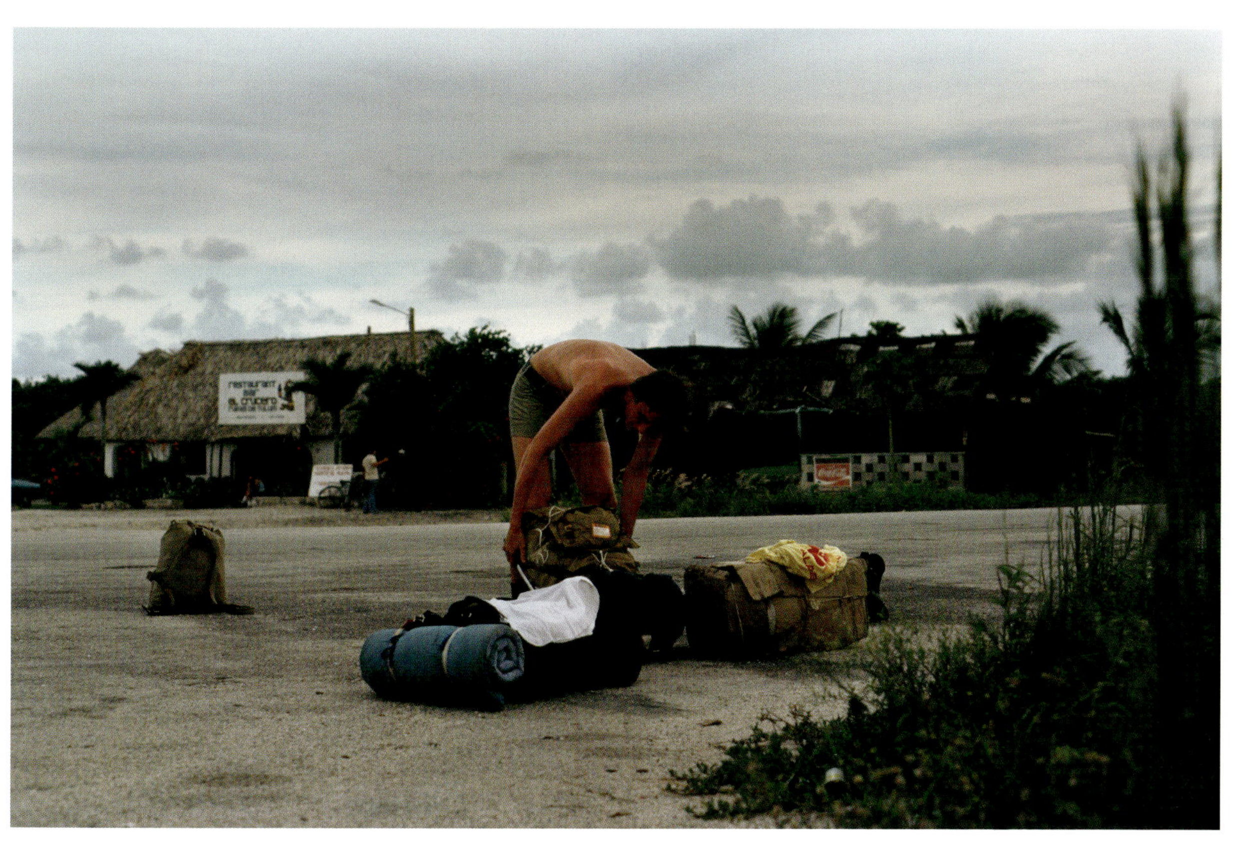

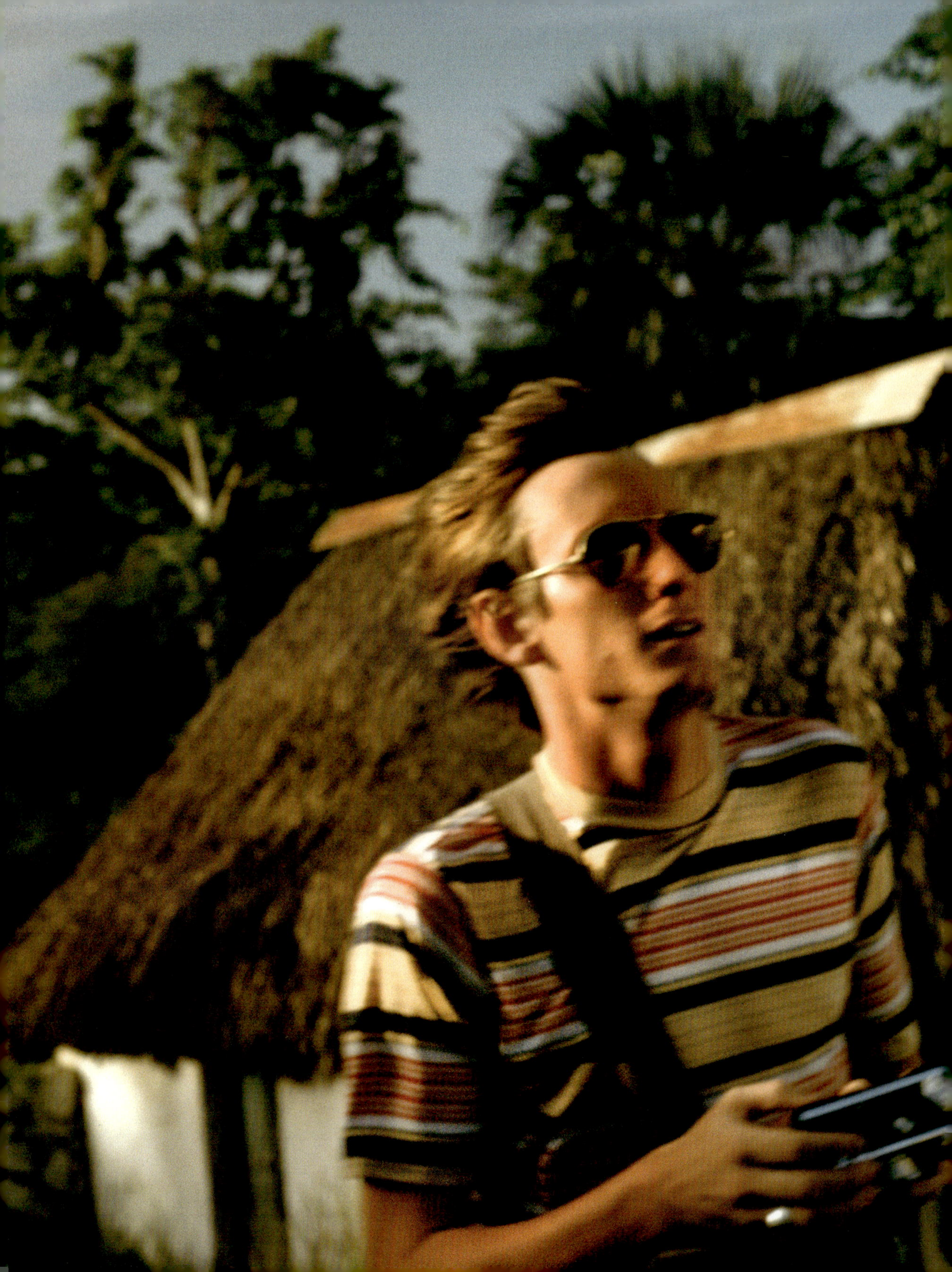

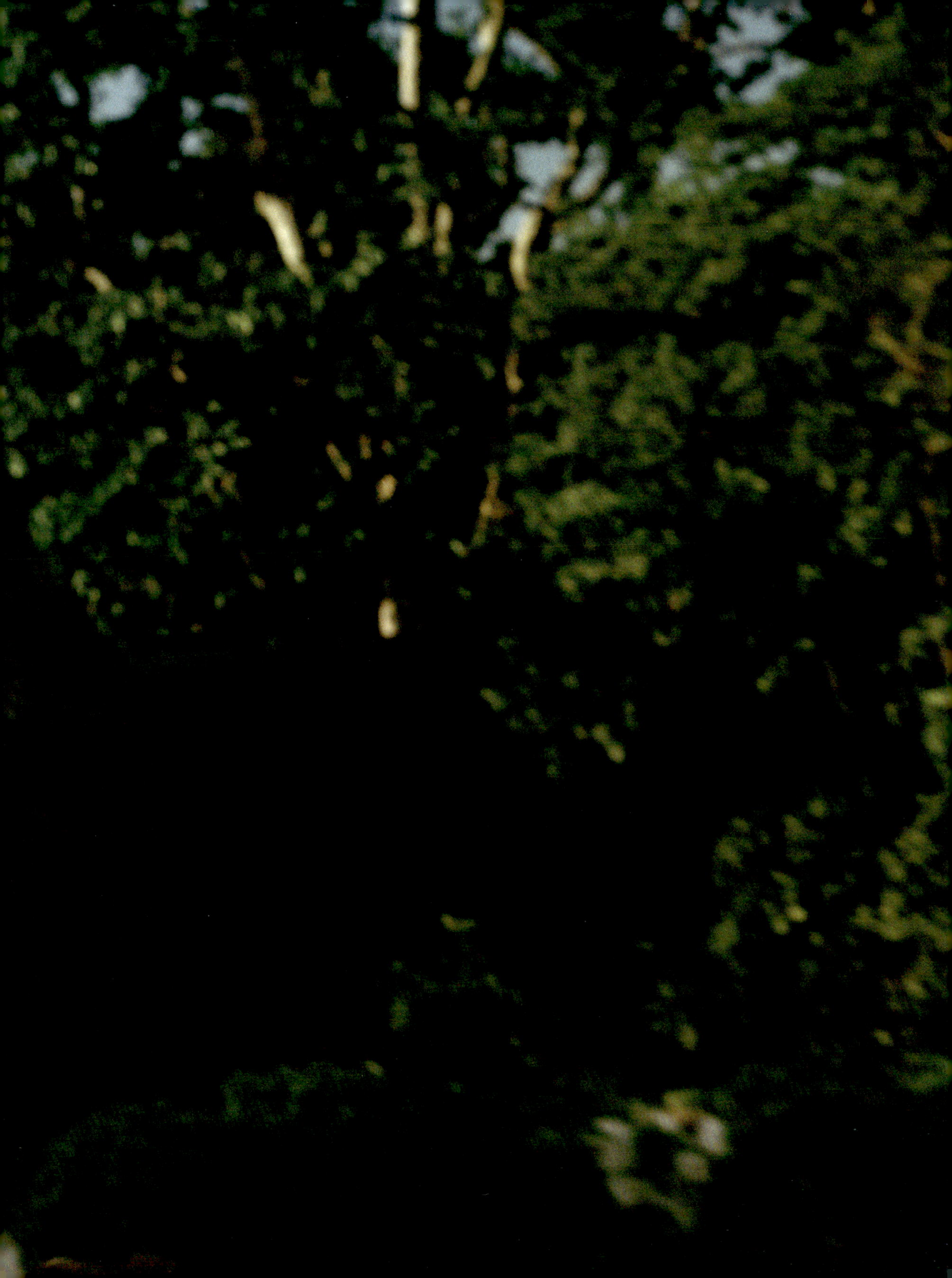

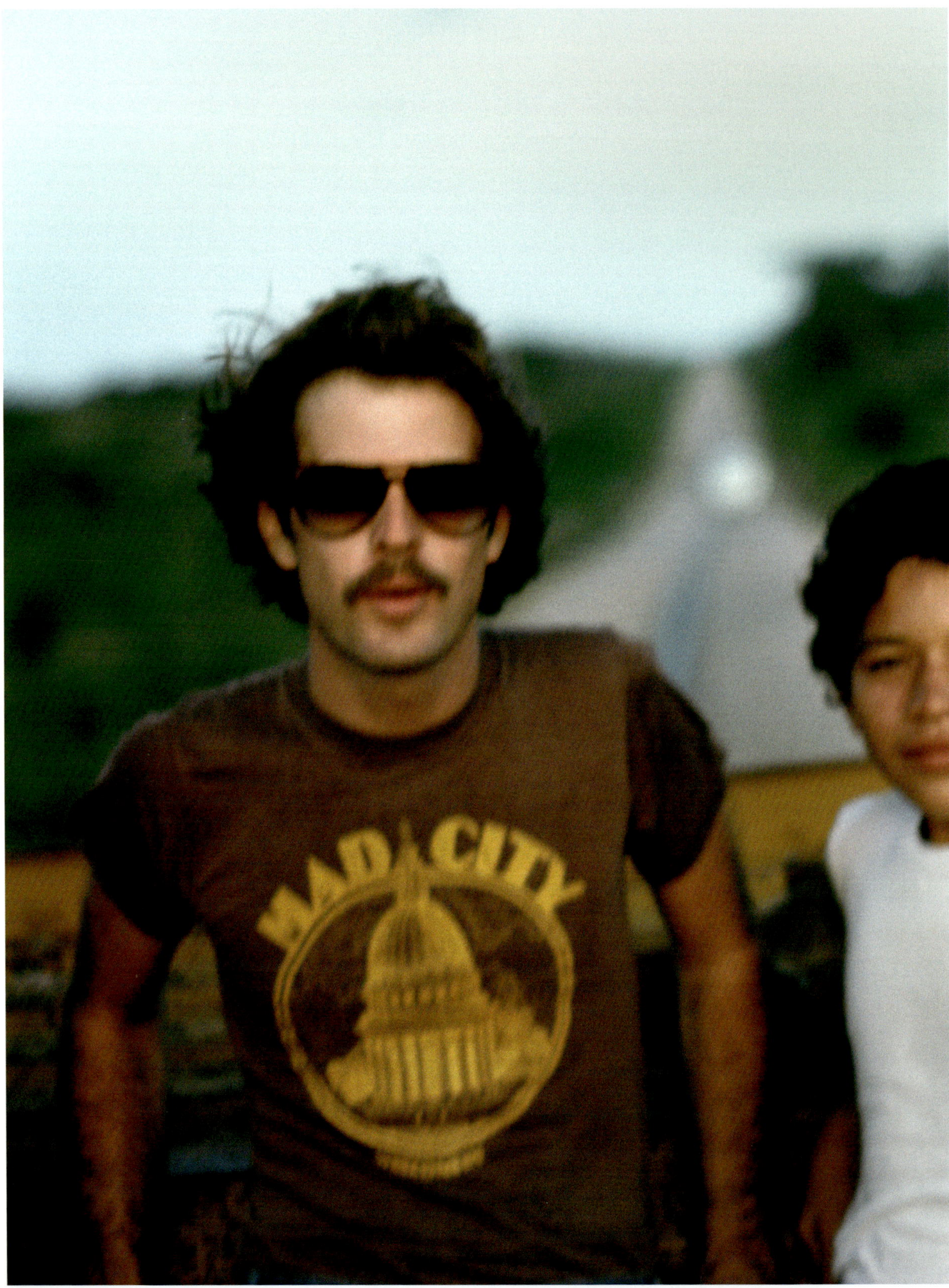

MAD CITY

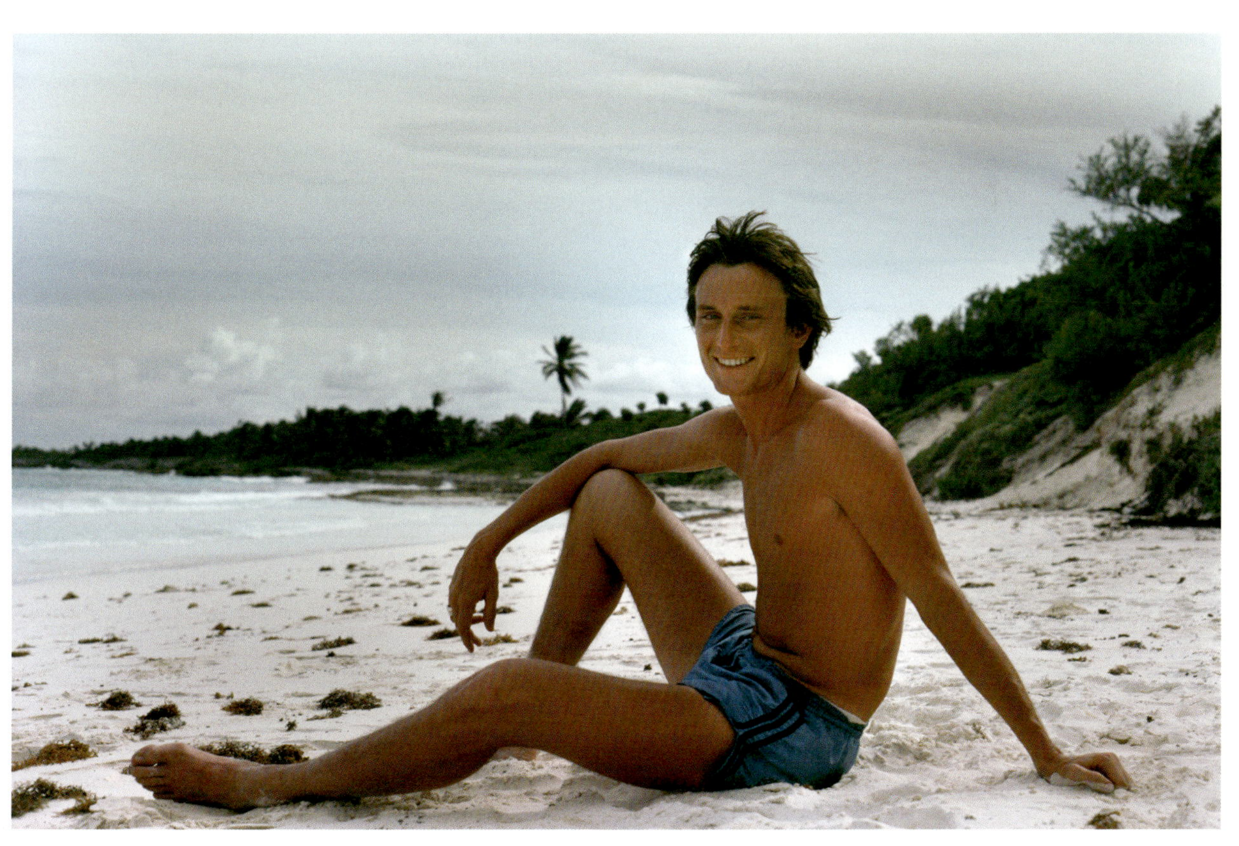

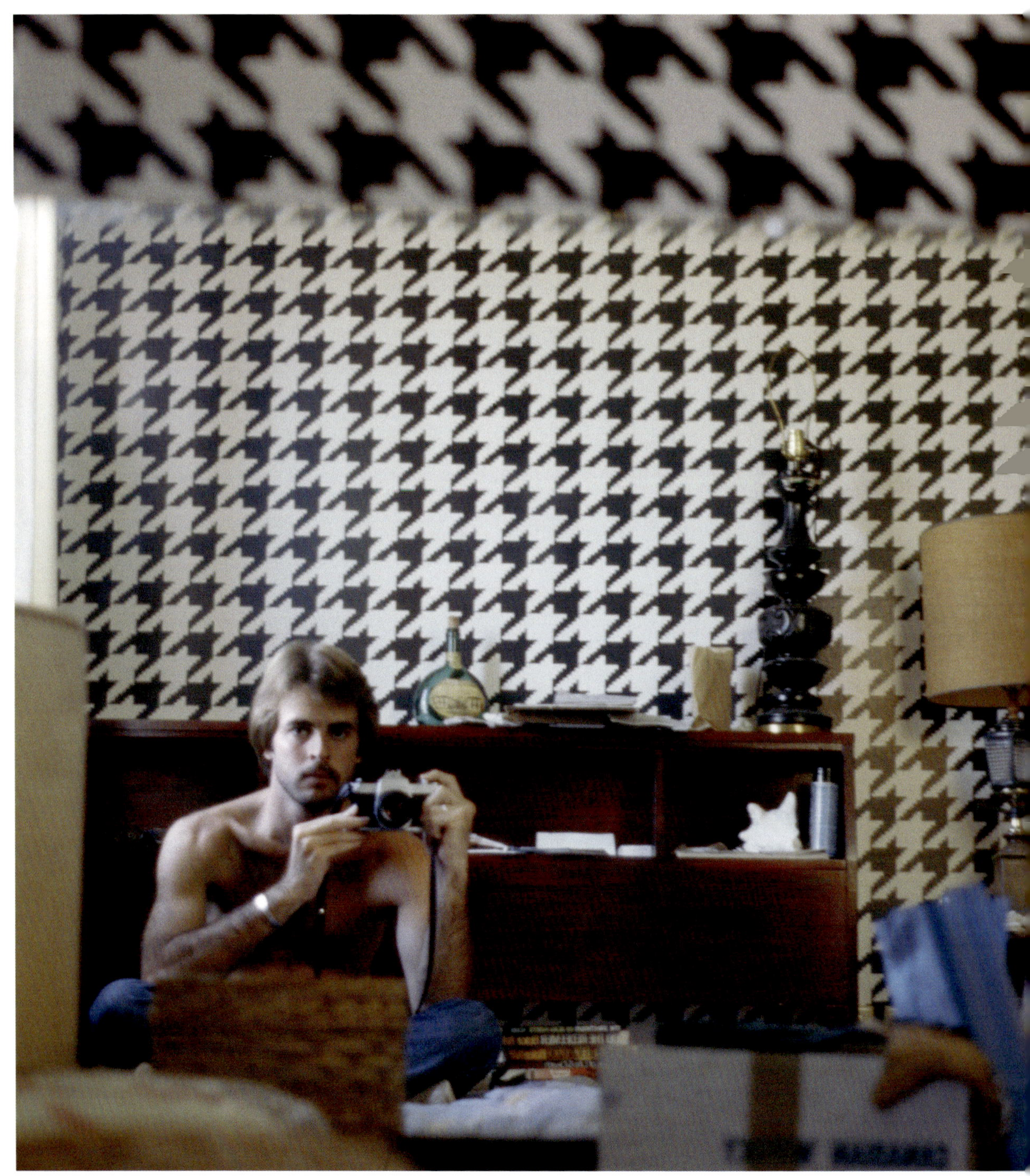

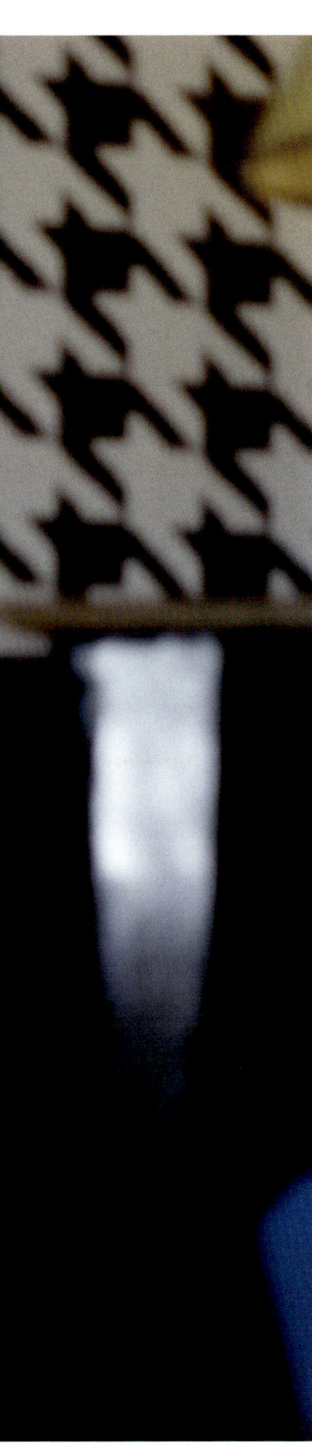

A while back, I found dusty boxes of kodachromes stored in my parent's house. I had not looked at the pictures in over 25 years, mainly because it was from a time I wanted to forget: my Jesus Days.

During my twenties, I was a youth minister for an evangelical Christian organization that had member chapters at secular colleges and universities across the U.S. It was my job to encourage young Christians in their faith. I listened to their problems, led Bible studies and prayer meetings, engaged in missions overseas and even took Jesus to the sunny beaches of Ft. Lauderdale, Florida during Spring Break.

As a boy, I had grown up in a Southern Baptist family in Kentucky. This born-again Christian world was as normal to me as bacon and eggs for breakfast. A missionary gave me a 35 mm camera in 1978 and I started to take pictures. They were not meant to be seen by anyone other than my friends and family. I photographed out of curiosity and the desire to capture a moment. Without my knowing it at the time, I realize that these pictures were my first artistic body of work. Looking at the images today, I see all my longing and wishes expressed, things I could not say in words.

To others, I appeared the model Christian, an evangelical poster boy. I prayed and read my bible, went to church and refrained from sex. But all through these days, I had a secret that I could not admit to others nor to myself. I loved but was not in love with the girl whom I thought I should marry and I was in love with my best friend with whom I never would have a relationship. I feared that if my secret was exposed, I would lose my family, my friends and my position. It would be the end of myself as I knew myself.

Compelled by my conflict of faith and homosexuality, I pursued counsel. A year and a half later, I broke up with my girlfriend, resigned from the Christian organization and came out as a gay man. During the summer of 1983, I moved to New York City where I entered Columbia University's Film School.

I became a photographer.

Front cover: Cedar Campus, Michigan

Inside cover: Cedar Campus, Michigan

1   Cedar Campus, Michigan

2   Greg and Todd, Kentucky

3   Brothers, Leslie (l) and Todd (r)

5   Lexington, Kentucky

6   Retreat, Eastern Kentucky

7   Tri State University, Angola, Indiana

8   Student, Purdue University, Indiana

10   First Apartment, Ft. Wayne, Indiana

11   Greg, Bible Study, Earlham College, Indiana

12   Sam, Auburn University at Montgomery, Alabama

14   Lake Wawasee, Indiana

15   Ft. Lauderdale, Florida

17   Oakwood Hotel, Lake Wawasee, Michigan

19   Bible Study, Lake Michigan, Indiana

20   Christian Bookstore, Louisville, KY

23   Vicki, Ft. Wayne, Indiana

24   Ft. Wayne, Indiana

25   Ft. Wayne, Indiana

26/27   Family, Lexington, Kentucky

29   Greg, Ft. Wayne, Indiana

30   Bus Station, Richmond, Indiana

31   Earlham College, Indiana

32   Mom and Dad, Lexington, KY

33   Student, Ball State University, Indiana

34   Greg, Louisville, Kentucky

36   Nursing Students, Ft. Wayne, Indiana

37   Louisville, Kentucky

38/39   Karen and Vicki (right). Ft. Wayne, Indiana

40   Greg, Camping, Georgia

41   Ft. Lauderdale, Florida

42   Ft. Lauderdale, Florida

43   Ft. Lauderdale, Florida

44/45   Ft. Lauderdale, Florida

46   Ft. Lauderdale, Florida

47   Ft. Lauderdale, Florida

68/49   Ft. Lauderdale, Florida

50   Worship and Praise, Ft. Lauderdale, Florida

51   Cedar Campus, Michigan

52/53   Christian Staff Volleyball, Lake Michigan, Michigan

54   John, Cedar Campus, Michigan

55   Students, Earlham College, Indiana

56/57   Church Couple, Ft. Wayne, Indiana

58   Dad, Lexington, Kentucky

59   Maternal Grandparents, Lexington, Kentucky

60/61   Kentucky

62   Paternal Grandmother, Lexington, KY

64   Berea College students, Planning Weekend, Kentucky

65   Mom, Lexington, Kentucky

67   Greg, 5 K, Ft. Wayne, Indiana

68/69   Vicki, Ft. Wayne, Indiana

70/71   Sam, Guatemala,

72   Sam, Bus Station, El Salvador

73   Sam, Yucatan. Mexico

74/75   Church, Guatemala City, Guatemala

76   Sam, Guatemala

77   Guatemala

78   Greg, Guatemala

79   Sam, Tulum, Mexico

80   Sam, Hitchhiking, Yucatan, Mexico

82   Greg, Hitchhiking, Yucatan, Mexico

83   Sam, Tulum, Mexico

84/85   Greg, Ft. Wayne, Indiana

Inside back cover: Tulum, Mexico

Back cover: Jesus One Way stamp